REIGNING CATS AND DOGS... DONKEYS, GOATS AND PIGS

Dr PAMELA DAVENPORT
ILLUSTRATED BY GEOFF GINN

**REIGNING CATS AND DOGS ...
DONKEYS, GOATS AND PIGS**

First published in Australia by Pamela Davenport 2022

A catalogue record for this
book is available from the
National Library of Australia

ISBN: 978-0-9751129-6-0 (pbk)
ISBN: 978-0-9751129-7-7 (ebk)

Text: © Pamela Davenport 2022
Illustrations: © Geoff Ginn 2022

Typesetting and design by Publicious Book Publishing
Published in collaboration with Publicious Book Publishing
www.publicious.com.au

No part of this book may be reproduced in any form, by photocopying or by any electronic or mechanical means, including information storage or retrieval systems, without permission in writing from both the copyright owner and the publisher of this book.

To the loving memory of my parents, Eric and Winifred Davenport, who shared and fostered my love of all creatures.

Contents

Acknowledgments

Foreword	i
Preface	iii
Chapter 1 . . . Dogs I have Known	1
Chapter 2 . . . For the Love of Cats	17
Chapter 3 . . . Nine Donkeys and One Horse	25
Chapter 4 . . . Three Sows and a Boar	45
Chapter 5 . . . Sheep to the Right, Goats to the Left	61
Chapter 6 . . . Brief Encounters	79
Postscript	91
About the Author	

Acknowledgements

I would like to acknowledge with gratitude the valuable contributions to this book by many people; first to Gen Johnston who typed the manuscript from the written version read to her over the phone; then to her mother, my dear friend Anne Young who proof-read and made some useful suggestions; to Geoff Ginn who created the delightful cartoons; to Barbara Merefield who provided the original French version of the poem about donkeys; to Trish who recently accepted my animals into her care and wrote tributes to Oliver and Bacchus; and to my friend Helen for her care of my animals and for her amusing anecdote.

I would like to acknowledge my vets, who were always professional and knowledgeable and who so often became friends. I speak especially of Mandy Roe, Kim Smith, Ranald Cameron, Richard Smith and Janine Dwyer.

My grateful thanks Heather Swaveley who came immediately to care for me and my animals when I became ill, and who encouraged my writing of this book.

Sincere thanks to my agent, Alex Adsett, who steers a safe passage between the Scylla of the publisher and the Charybdis of my desires.

And finally, to Denis, Shaun Fitzpatrick, John Turner, Doug and to my wonderful Dad, all of whom built animal houses, strong fences and guinea pig hutches. Thank you for your patience, kindness and expertise.

Thank you all.

Pamela Davenport

Foreword

These stories of Pamela's animals paint a delightful picture of her love of animals and of ancient history in one book.

As one of Pamela's oldest school friends from Somerville House, I enjoyed visiting Pamela at Kuraby and even had the responsibility of caring for her animals for a short time. Many of Pamela's friends who also stepped in when Pamela had to be elsewhere, would agree that a detailed description of what, when and where to feed each animal showed the care and attention which kept them all so healthy.

Pamela also deserves a description. My children thought that Pamela's tall and statuesque figure and long blonde braids made her appear like a Roman aristocrat. I'm sure many of her students would have thought the same. Her house with its white columns on a hill surrounded by animal paddocks and stately trees reminds me of a Roman villa - a fitting backdrop to her stories.

Anne Young

Preface

"For better or worse, in sickness and in health."

These words, taken from the promise made in the marriage service, sum up my attitude to the responsibilities when I accept the care of an animal. I have always loved animals (except cockroaches!). More of that later. My love of animals sprang from my parents' love of all creatures, and their determination to do the very best for them. I have had numerous animals in my life, many of them adopted from animal shelters, or rescued from a life of abuse, hunger or illness. I have had dogs of many breeds, cats, horses, pigs, goats, sheep and donkeys (which I bred and whose offspring I reluctantly sold). I have had a pet possum who visited for his morning feed, and rescued spiders when they were trapped in the house. Having set them free, I always avoid damaging spider's webs outside. I have done 'mouth to beak' on a drowning rooster and on birds hit by cars.

    I worked long days as a teacher and later as a writer, archaeologist and historian. I enjoyed the company of my first dog at Kuraby, Dante, and the other animals when at home. The animals had full run of my 5-acre property, which was initially surrounded by bushland that was later developed into houses and apartments, although I have maintained most of my acreage. When I had all my animals, the many trees provided shade and the area set aside for the grazing animals was lush grass. The remainder of the property was open for the animals to explore. In the present time, I no longer have most of my animals, but the winding driveway still becomes a waterfall in heavy rain. At the top of the driveway is the house, with the animal enclosures nearby.

The stories of my animals, some amusing and some sad, are the subject of this book. The combination of animal anecdotes and Ancient Roman tales will tear at the heartstrings of both young and mature adults. Enjoy!

"Until one had loved an animal, some parts of one remained unawakened."

Anatole France

Chapter 1

Dogs I have Known

"Gentlemen of the jury, the one absolutely unselfish friend that remains in this selfish world, that never deserts him, the one that never proves ungrateful or treacherous, is his dog."
Senator George Graham Vest

It seems inevitable that, of the many types of animals I have loved, it was a dog I loved first, and I would eventually have a dozen dogs over the years. My mother told me that as soon as I could toddle, I launched myself fearlessly at any dog I saw. So Tony, a curly-coated retriever, was an appropriate second birthday gift to me from a friend of my mother, in 1939.

That same friend gave the gift of a dog to my mother when she lived in Kin Kin in the 1920s. He was an English bulldog called Robert Bruce, a singularly inappropriate name for that most British of breeds. I have a portrait of him, painted by my mother, on my wall. Robert Bruce lived for many years because breeders had not yet produced this breed with pushed-in faces, that led to breathing difficulties and a lifespan of about four years. This sort of interference is unconscionable. He finally died in the only vet surgery in Brisbane, where the City Hall now stands.

Tony was a wonderful choice. "That breed is good with children," said my Mum's friend who gave him to me at our house in Moorooka. He was absolutely devoted to me and he was so protective. He would not allow anyone to touch me except my family or Uncle Leslie, my mother's brother. Anyone else, he would have eaten alive. A neighbour, in Dad's presence, lifted me up and Tony flew up and bit his arm.

I used to wander down into the bush and have picnics and walks with Tony. On one notable occasion we went to the abandoned tannery which was still full of water and chemicals. Tony slipped in and could not get out. I rushed to ask Dad to help and he rescued him. Tony was dyed dark red for several months.

Tony had a friend called Terry from next door, a terrier whom he loved. They were inseparable. If we went anywhere there was water, Tony of course plunged in. Dad used to take us to the Brisbane River. Terry was not such a strong swimmer and when he tired, he used to tuck his front paws under Tony's collar and be towed along. Tony did not mind. Then one day I found Terry under the Jacaranda tree dying; he had been poisoned. I was heartbroken and so was Tony.

In Tony's youth, my mother was heard to say, "If there is anything wooden, Tony has chewed it." Everything had his teeth marks on it, even the house stumps. If Mum was weeding and put a tool down, he quickly buried it, to be found many years later.

Tony was very interested in food. For breakfast he had bread and milk and for dinner, heart. When there was no heart my mother gave up her meat ration so Tony would not go short. This was during the war when meat was rationed. Mum always cooked it because she thought people would be less likely to go to the trouble of putting poison in cooked meat. Tony would not eat raw meat. One time, the butcher had no heart so he sent something else. Tony sniffed it delicately and decided it was not for him, so he picked up his dish and tipped it under the hedge. I thought that was very funny and quite perceptive.

In spite of Tony's rejection of the meal which was not heart, he was interested in most food which was "forbidden fruit". On Mondays but on no other day, he crossed Ipswich Road to the Ayres' house, where the stale cakes were set aside for him. He regularly visited the corner shop, where out-of-date sausages were saved for him. On one occasion, he arrived home proudly carrying a whole Windsor sausage – I was always apologising for Tony – we thought he had stolen it. I will never forget the sight of Tony with the Windsor sausage protruding from either side of his mouth, bouncing along looking so proud of himself. All was well; it was a legitimate trophy. However, the lunches of no tradesmen, electricians and road workers were safe. I was sent to apologise, often with a replacement repast probably more tasty than the original.

The most terrifying event in Tony's life occurred around 1942, when American troops were stationed in Brisbane and surrounding districts. According to neighbours who saw the incident, a U.S. Army truck pulled up and Tony was snatched from the footpath. We were all distraught. Mum phoned for information, but to no avail. Although he had identification, it was ignored. American troops had been known to sometimes seize dogs as mascots and then abandon them when they moved on. Tony arrived home about a week later, gravel-rashed and with cut feet. He must have jumped from the truck and made his way home. This, I think, has coloured my view of Americans ever since! There were several military bases near our area, but I suspect the one he escaped from was Beaudesert, so he probably made his way home from this more distant outpost.

Tony lived to the age of sixteen, a great age for a large dog. I was eighteen in January 1955 when, at the height of summer, he started lapsing into unconsciousness in the afternoons. Normally, when it became cool, he awoke for his tea, but a few weeks later, one day he did not wake and we were so sad. Dad wrapped him for burial in the woollen jacket Mum had bought for him when he was in hospital. It was a knitted jacket that had been mended many times and although Dad would never part with it, he gave it up for Tony. I had never seen Dad weep before.

Tony was an absolutely wonderful dog and I still think of him with so much affection. That was my experience with my dog Tony.

Although I had a number of cats, a rabbit and guinea pigs, there was no other dog in my life until Christmas Eve 1963, when my then husband and I went to the RSPCA shelter in Fairfield. I, of course, wanted to take all the dogs home, especially one very elderly sick dog, but my husband said we could not take that dog; he would not live, so I reluctantly chose just one - a small, young dog of mixed breed, with long hair and spotted tan markings. I called him Dante and he lived for many years and was a constant delight. All the other animals loved him; he was so gentle and protective.

On Christmas Day, the day after we had adopted him, Dante became seriously ill with what I thought was distemper and he had a visit from the vet instead of from Santa Claus. He did recover, surrounded by the good company of all the other animals. I could safely leave him with my illegal rabbit and the guinea pigs. One morning I looked out to see Violetta the donkey and Roger the goat, led by Dante. They had been exploring Kuraby, my suburb, but decided the outside world was too scary and quickly returned home in procession. As soon as possible, I built new fences to discourage further expeditions. Dante accepted all the other animals, but his favourite was a cat, whom I named Beatrice. I saw her, ill and very pregnant, at the Kuraby School where Mum and I went to vote.

One perceptive and endearing aspect of Dante's life was weekly, when the programme 'Better Homes and Gardens' was on the television. As soon as the music to introduce the segment featuring the vet Dr Harry Cooper played, Dante rushed in and sat to watch the whole segment, seated in front of the television. He enjoyed seeing the whole variety of animals.

When Dante was very old, he developed doggy dementia, so I used to take him each morning for Mum to dog-sit and as company for Mum's two dogs, Jonathon and Michal. Dante had a Valium each morning because he used to howl. One day, however, he jumped Mum's fence, which he had never done before. I searched for him for days and I finally went to the RSPCA Shelter and as I arrived, there he was, being carried on a stretcher, having been hit by a car. My vet was able to help him and he lived happily for another year. He was almost thirteen when he died, in about 1976.

In the meantime, I acquired Ramona and Sheba in the late 1970s, so then I had three dogs. I noticed an advertisement for a curly-coated retriever for sale, and could not resist. Ramona was liver-coloured, but in so many ways just like Tony, especially in her gentle nature.

One day a Kelpie cross arrived at my door, whom I named Sheba. She was very friendly and cheerful and looked in fairly good condition. I thought she was the dog that my neighbour had lost a few weeks before, but he denied that she was his dog. What could I do but adopt her? She proved a good mate for Ramona and it was a lovely sight when Mum and I took our dogs to the doggy beach in Moreton Bay. The only dog which did not plunge in and have a lovely time was Dante. Sheba used to try to keep up with Ramona, and Mum's dogs paddled to their bellies rather than swim. Originally curly-coated retrievers were bred to fetch shot game like ducks, back to the shooter. I had Sheba for many years, but Ramona sadly died from cancer of the jaw after only two years, she was only 3 or 4 when I got her.

At the estimated age of ten Sheba tore two cruciate ligaments in her back legs, one after the other, chasing my neighbour's horse, a game the horse seemed to enjoy. Although both legs were expertly repaired by my vet, arthritis set in and walking was impossible. I had to make the difficult decision to euthanise her because her quality of life was non-existent and 'euthanasia' means kindly death.

My mother, when she died in 1984, had only Michal after the death of her other dog Jonathan. Michal was a little terrier she had rescued from the street in Sunnybank. I cared for Michal at her home for a couple of years till she died at what I suspected an advanced age.

Other dogs I had loved and rescued for various reasons included Sherlock and Agatha (Christie) the bloodhounds. The RSPCA asked the public to give a home to these abandoned animals. I answered the call, although I still had Sheba. Unfortunately, Agatha was an escape artist and I feared she would be run over on the road, so she was returned to the RSPCA after a few days and they rehomed her. Sherlock loved to run in the adjoining bushland but I had to keep him on a lead, lest he too, nose to the ground and fixated on beguiling smells, should run into danger. After a year or so he became very ill. I rushed him to the vet, who was a very fine surgeon. His gut had twisted and although the operation was successful, he died two nights later in the vet hospital. I learned then, that deep-chested dogs should not be fed a meal for a half hour before or after exercise. It was a bitter lesson, one which I wish I had been told about earlier. I missed Sherlock very much.

Yet another curly-coated retriever was advertised for sale in the paper, and yes, you have guessed it, I bought her. I called her Charlotte. She looked like Tony with Victorian curls and liquid brown eyes. I still had Sherlock when Charlotte arrived, but lost him soon afterwards. Charlotte and Sheba soon became best friends though.

The gap of Sherlock was soon filled by Munya, an English collie. A friend was helping rehome dogs in bad environments. Munya is Spanish for 'beautiful' and she was certainly a lovely creature but had been shockingly neglected. Her original owner was Spanish and when she returned to Spain, Munya was given to her sister. She was never allowed inside the house and was forced to sleep on the cement patio. Then she was given to her father, who treated her in the same way.

When I adopted her, she had the most painful, crippling arthritis. I had to help and a vet specialising in acupuncture came to the house every week to treat her. She was so happy and I could see the gratitude in her eyes. I knew she would deteriorate but at least her suffering was relieved. She slept on a trampoline bed with a comfortable foam mattress on top and a rug at night. She survived one winter but the vet and I noticed at times it was increasingly difficult for her to stand. A painful but necessary decision was made to euthanise her. I wished I had known of her plight earlier.

I still had Charlotte; lively, enthusiastic and active. She was quite old, about ten, when she became very ill with a problem for which she required extensive surgery. The vet, not my usual one, said, "At her age, she will never survive the surgery, so better to euthanise her." My reply was, "Give her a chance. If she dies under the anaesthetic she will not have suffered." The operation was successful and she lived another three happy years dying at thirteen, an escapee from the scalpel. Her death when it came, was peaceful, from old age. Sheba lived to about 17 years old, and Charlotte passed away about a year later.

During Charlotte's later years, I adopted another dog from the RSPCA but I could not bear to visit the shelter, choosing one dog from amongst all those eager, hopeful faces. I asked the RSPCA legacy officer to choose a suitable pet for me. She chose a dog which was predominately Shetland sheep dog, so I named him Ossian, after a character in a Scottish Island epic. He had long brown fur, pointed nose and alert, pointed ears. The two dogs were great company. One day, Ossian gave a sharp bark and his eye clouded over. I took him to the specialist ophthalmologist, Richard. Although he could do nothing for the damaged eye, he was able to save the sight of Ossian's left eye. Ossian loved Richard and I think he looked forward to seeing him on follow-up visits. The endearing part of this relationship was that, when Richard phoned to ask about Ossian's progress, the dog could always recognise his voice. When I put the phone to Ossian's ears, he pricked his ears and gave a bark of excitement. I enjoyed Ossian's gentle company for only a few years. He became ill with pancreatitis, and in spite of heroic efforts by Richard and the other vets, he succumbed in 2002.

While I was overseas, Danni arrived on the scene. My friend, who was looking after the beasties, could not approach him, but left food and water out. Meanwhile, she became attached to the donkeys and spent every night with them, guarding them fiercely if any stray dogs appeared. She was a delightful little red cattle dog. Eventually I was able to approach her and she became part of the family. I had her spayed and discovered that Danny was a female, so changed her name to Danni. She was happy to stay on the couch with me in the evenings. As I prepared for bed, she wanted to join the donkeys. If I came home late, I saw four pairs of eyes glowing in the headlights.

Danni was terrified of storms, so I spent considerable money to have chain wire installed around the whole property, to stop her heedlessly running in a storm. If I was home, she would come to the house for protection, but one day I was out showing my English cousin Brisbane. Frantic with fear, she dug under the chain wire, and ran across busy Beenleigh Road, where she was killed instantly according to neighbours who notified me. If only I had been home, I might have her company now.

Soon after Danni died in 2008, another curly-coated retriever entered my life, Robbie. His owner and her husband trained obedience dogs and Robbie had won many prizes in that area. His living conditions were not ideal – a small enclosed box on stilts about five metres square – and while I do not know how often he was allowed to run free, I suspect very rarely. I bought Robbie and he found his way into my heart immediately. He was allowed to run free on the property and I had young friends who took him to the dog park as well.

I also adopted Rollo, a small poodle cross in around 2010. His name was chosen because it was a medieval French dog's name. He had been returned to the RSPCA because he had jumped up when the owners had held up their two-year-old child by her legs above his head. Their stupidity was unbelievable. A few days later they came to reclaim him but the staff at the shelter refused, saying they were not suitable owners. My friend, the donor officer, asked if I would have him and I was happy to help. He and Robbie were great mates. Robbie, like all my retrievers, was a delight. I was so sad when one night in 2017 he could not stand. I managed to get him to the emergency department of the Veterinary Specialist Centre. The next morning, he was transferred to the main hospital. Nick the vet administered every possible test and my friend the acupuncture vet visited every day. Finally, a scan indicated that he had inoperable cancer of the spine. The decision was inevitable. He was only nine years old.

Rollo lived happily to around the age of eleven. After Robbie died, Rollo was on his own for three years and was very lonely. My health had deteriorated to such an extent that I was unable to take responsibility for the care of another dog. Rollo had been a healthy little bloke but while I was in hospital, he became ill and his kidneys were failing. The vet tried to rehydrate him with an intravenous drip, but he was dying. I was determined he was not going to die in a strange place so I persuaded the doctor to allow me to go home. On that last night I slept on the couch with my hand on his head. He lay on his familiar bed. In the morning I carried him into the kitchen and he knew he was home and seemed at peace. At 12:30pm the vet came to euthanise him. It was upsetting because all his veins had collapsed and only heavy sedation was effective. At least he slipped away hearing my loving last words. This was only about a year ago in 2020.

My dogs, of whatever breed, and however long I had cared for them, were all dear to me and each had a special place in my heart.

Pamela's home shared with her animals

A portrait painted by Pamela's mother, Winifred Davenport, of her English bulldog named Robert Bruce

Tony, the curly coated retriever and Terry the terrier with Pamela at 11 years old, in 1948

Tony in old age, with Pamela

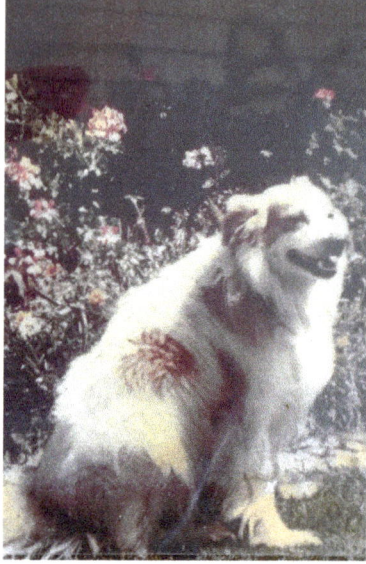
Dante, a mixed breed dog who was Pamela's first dog after Tony

Pamela and her dogs Sheba the Kelpie cross, Charlotte the curly-coated retriever and Dante, with Bunter the sheep

"Don't leave me out, Mum."

Charlotte the curly-coated retriever, ready for action

Pamela and her mother's dogs, Jonathan and Michal – mixed breed terriers with Biblical names

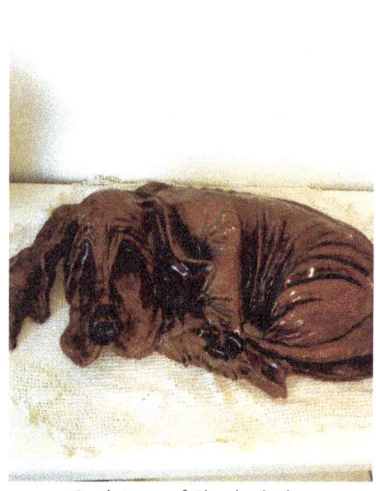

Sculpture of Sherlock the bloodhound, gifted to Pamela by one of her students

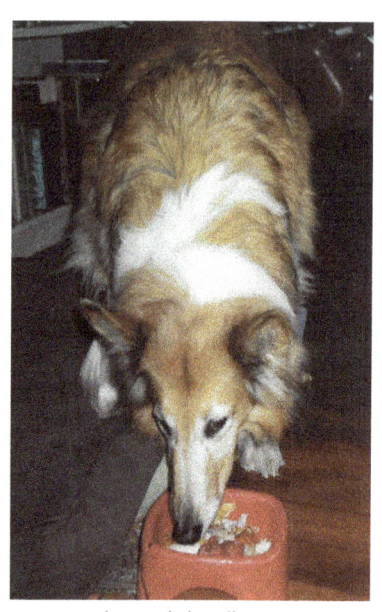

Munya the English collie, tucking in

Danni the red cattle dog
How quiet she looks

Rollo the small poodle cross. "The grass is as high as an elephant's eye."

Danni in her role as donkey protector

Rollo and Robbie, homeward bound

Rollo and Robbie. A long walk deserves a good rest.

Bedtime story

Chapter 2

For the Love of Cats

"Owners of dogs will have noticed that, if you provide them with food and water and shelter and affection, they will think you are God, whereas owners of cats are compelled to realise that, if you provide them with food and water and affection, they draw the conclusion that they are God."

Christopher Hitchens

My great-grandmother, according to my mother, was an irascible old lady, who had a cat of which she was inordinately fond. My mother, of course, wanted to pat it but it was apparently as bad-tempered as its owner. Nana, my grandmother, while never unkind, took no interest in animals. I do not know where my mother acquired her love of cats or dogs. My father's family also had always at least one cat as well as dogs.

My first cat, a black cat, was rescued from a tree by Dad using a long ladder. I was into Roman names then, and called him Brutus. Tony was still alive and in his youth would not have allowed us to share our affection with a cat. In his old age, however, he tolerated Brutus. Perhaps the cat's exuberance reminded Tony of his youth. In days before it was considered wise to keep cats inside at night, Nana put Brutus out and he was killed on the road. He had been neutered but seemed still to have had the urge to visit a female across Ipswich Road. No subsequent cats were ever allowed out at night. They had beds under the house and my ever-patient father's task was to put them to bed.

After Brutus came Hector, Aeneas, Paris and Cassandra, all rescued from difficult environments. I was reading Homer's 'Iliad' and was enamoured with the Trojans, hence the names. Hector was a fluffy grey Persian, while Aeneas was a tabby, and Paris a feisty ginger. Cassandra, the only female, was a tortoiseshell. Most of my cats were moggies of indeterminate breed and of various colours. I was living at home then but though they were considered my cats, my parents loved them and continued to care for them after I left home.

I remember Dad combing the neighbourhood for hours until he found Hector, caught in a fence, crying pitifully, with a severely injured spine. After treatment he was able to walk but was always crippled. Our neighbour, an Ocker male with no sympathy for animals, was scornful of Dad's concern, but I know whose attitude I preferred.

Cassandra as a kitten had rickets, a very painful condition which affected the bones. Our vet treated her with injections and dietary supplements but she gradually lost most of her teeth. Our vet was unavailable so we called a vet whom we would never let darken our door again. He ordered her a diet of meat saying it would alleviate her rickets (which she no longer had). Mum, frustrated, said, "But she has no teeth to chew meat." Cassandra lived to a comfortable old age with soft food and lots of loving care.

There was a joke in our house that, when some activity such as changing the station on the radio was required, someone, usually Mum, would say to Dad or to me, "Would you mind getting up, I have a cat on my knee?" There was always a cat on somebody's knee so it was a good excuse.

All these cats died at intervals and peacefully of the illnesses of old age.

My first cat at Kuraby was Beatrice, rescued by Mum and me from the voting station at the local school. Dante completely fell in love with her. After she recovered from her cat flu, she gave birth to three black kittens just like her. In the old house where I lived before the new one was built, there was a couch in the kitchen and I placed a box there for her. Dante kept gazing at her with interest and concern. Beatrice picked up each kitten and placed it in front of him on the floor. Dante licked each one and Beatrice looked on with approval. I kept one kitten and found homes for the other two. Dante and Beatrice remained inseparable until Beatrice at an advanced age died from kidney failure, one of the most common diseases in cats.

After Beatrice, cats came thick and fast. Some, no doubt, were alerted to the possibility of food by the Kuraby feline network; others were thrust upon me by friends or were rescued from difficult situations. There were too many to count.

One of these was Nelson, so named by me because he had only one eye. He was haunting the school grounds, fed surreptitiously by the students. The housekeeper, a very bitter woman who loved only her pot plants, was about to send him to be euthanised when I intervened. I took him to the vet who attended to his infected eye, and Nelson took up residence at Winifred Street.

Then came Cuppa, named because of his love for milky tea. He belonged to my former history teacher and later colleague. She asked that, if anything happened to her, would I give Cuppa a home? I promised and when her housekeeper phoned to say that Miss Morgan was very ill, but would not go into hospital until she knew I would come for the cat. I left immediately and collected Cuppa, then went to tell his owner that I had him safely in care. I remember saying that I would bring him back to her when she was well again. "I am not going to get well Pamela." Sadly, she was right. Miss

Morgan died two or three days later. Cuppa lived for many years, dying of cancer of the nose and mouth.

Then there was Micky, who was already named. The intention was that he was to stay only until his owner left hospital, but his owner was admitted to a nursing home. I took Micky to visit his owner several times until he died, after which Micky became a permanent resident.

Then came a group of cats with Egyptian names. I thought this appropriate because the Egyptians loved and admired cats. They protected Egyptians from scorpions, venomous snakes and their precious grain supplies from the depredations from mice. Cats were often depicted helping their owners hunting.

From the Second Dynasty (c3000BC), cats were deified. Bastet was the chief cat goddess, worshipped at Bubastis, in the north east of Egypt, and later throughout the country. Pet cats were often buried with great ceremony after mummification. According to some later Ancient Greek writers, a person who kills a cat purposely could be put to death or, if it was accidental, then the eyebrows of the culprit would be shaved. It is no wonder, then, that my first cat with an Egyptian name was Bastet, a glossy black short-haired moggie, who was matriarch of the cats for many years.

Horus, named after the god of the sky, often depicted as a falcon, was a beautiful black Persian, thrust at me through the window by a young woman who was known for her eccentric behaviour, the manifestation of which often involved the stealing of cats. After thrusting Horus through the window, she fled. She was obviously somebody's pet, so I put advertisements in the local paper and in the windows of local shops with no success. So Horus joined the household. In his old age, he contracted a disease which required daily injections, a procedure which he tolerated but did not enjoy. He finally succumbed and died peacefully.

Set, named after the rather unpopular god of the inhospitable desert, was feisty and curious, a trait which led him to go exploring one day. He was hit by a car in broad daylight. My neighbour buried him before he told me. While I realised that he did it not to upset me, I wanted closure. I always hoped it was not Set and that he would come home.

Isis, Nut, Sekhmet and Osiris, all lived comfortable, unremarkable lives, dying at advanced ages; most of them succumbing to that enemy of cats, kidney disease. They all lived happily together, which is fairly unusual for so many cats living in close proximity. Fortunately, a greater knowledge of the causes of kidney disease in cats and a specialised diet has allowed vets and owners to keep the disease under control for longer.

Sekhmet did not live up to her name, as the fierce goddess depicted as a woman with a lion's head. Sekhmet was rather a shy cat, initially hiding from my friend Helen, who was caring for my animals when I was away, accompanying my archaeologist friend on the Ghan to Alice Springs. Once Helen gained Sekhmet's trust, she and Helen became very close. Despite this, while I was away, Sekhmet became very ill at the advanced age of twenty-three. She was admitted to the Veterinary Specialist Centre. The vet phoned me and I asked if he could keep her alive so I could say goodbye. Good as his word, when I went to see Sekhmet, she was on a drip but still alive. The vet was in tears as he gave her the lethal injection, saying that he had never had to say goodbye to such an old girl. As was my habit with all my animals, I talked to her, so the last sound she heard was my voice to comfort her.

A school colleague asked me to take her mother's Siamese cat, called, I think, Shah. He was a beautiful creature but my colleague feared her mother might trip over him. She was very frail. I did so, though her mother wanted to keep the cat, and I understood that. Her daughter was adamant. Unfortunately, soon I after I accepted him, the cat was diagnosed with diabetes. I struggled to stabilise him, but he deteriorated. In spite of all the vet's efforts and at considerable cost, I had to say goodbye.

My last cat, and she will be my last, because of my deteriorating health, is Neith, the Egyptian goddess of hunting. In spite of her name, she does not get the opportunity to hunt. Neith is an inside cat and seems quite contented to be so. I adopted her from a former student, a vet, who found her abandoned as a very young kitten. In her early years she was exuberant and rather unpredictable. Some of her characteristics seemed to indicate that her mother may have been a wild cat.

Now, however, it would be hard to find a more gentle, contented cat. Neith has three or four places to sleep and alternates between them. My bed is the favourite, as well as under the bed, on the floor in front of the heater in winter and the fan in summer, and on the couch in the study, especially when I am watching TV. Neith is nearly fifteen. She has regular Catlax to ward off furball and loves to lick it from the tube. She is wonderful company for me since I live alone. One of her most endearing habits is to put her paw on my arm when she wants to attract my attention. Should I die before her, she will be adopted by a cat-loving friend, who visits her regularly to make friends. Although that adage may be true in some cases, that 'a dog has a master, a cat has a servant', most of my cats have treated me as an equal!!

"I love cats because I enjoy my home, and little by little they become its visible soul."

Jean-Cocteau

Cats at work, on top of the septic tank at Kuraby

Cats still at work, in the kitchen

Bastet looking just like her namesake, the chief Egyptian cat goddess of Bubastis

Neith, the Egyptian goddess of hunting, who never gets a chance to hunt

Neith, looking angelic in her moggie splendour

Chapter 3

Nine Donkeys and One Horse

Nine Donkeys

When I come to enter paradise, The country of the good God, I will say: 'Come, friends of the blue sky, Poor sweet beasts who, with a brusque movement of the ear, Chase the houseflies, the blowflies and the bees'.

> Translation by Pamela Davenport of part of the poem, 'Pray to go to Paradise with the Donkeys' by Francis Jammes See Appendix for the original French poem and full English translation.

There is no more erroneous opinion, often stated with conviction, that 'donkeys are stubborn and stupid'. On the contrary, they are gentle, intelligent and eminently biddable, when they can see the sense in what is being asked of them.

I do not think I had seen a donkey before I visited England, but I loved the book 'The Small One' by Paul Gallico. I fell in love with donkeys on the English beaches, where they spent long patient hours giving rides to children. Donkeys had often been derided and treated with incredible cruelty in Europe, where they are just pack animals. In Spain, until recently, during an annual religious ceremony, a donkey was loaded until its back was broken. The donkey was believed to be taking on the sins of all humans, as Jesus did. Similarly, in Biblical times a goat was driven into the wilderness to take away human sin, hence the term 'scapegoat'.

When my husband and I moved to Kuraby in about 1964, he, knowing of my desire for a donkey, was able to trace one and she was delivered, much to my delight. Since she was unnamed, I called her Violetta, after the donkey in 'The Small One'. She was a beautiful creature, white with a fine conformation. Although infrequently handled, she was quick to learn and eager to please.

She was always hungry and, hearing that molasses was a helpful dietary supplement to add to her normal food of pony pellets and lucerne chaff, we bought some. What we did not know was that, if contaminated with water, it becomes dangerous. Violetta loved the molasses, but a few days later she became ill and the vet was called. This was before the Kessels Road Vet Hospital was opened, where we came to know Kim Smith, my large animal vet for twenty-five years. The vet who came was another who would never darken the door again. We told him Violetta had eaten molasses and thought it had smelt strange, but he did not know the significance, as we did not, but we were not vets. Violetta died a painful death with what we later learned was lactic acid poisoning. It was a bitter lesson and molasses was never again offered to my donkeys.

My experience with Violetta over that year had not dampened my longing for a donkey. When I heard of a jack donkey for sale during the Brisbane Exhibition in 1965, he was ours! My husband collected him in a trailer with a cage attached and Dominic, as I called him, arrived at Winifred Street. He was small, only about eight hands (about 48 inches) at the shoulder, and was grey and white. His coat was short, even in winter.

He had been handled but not trained. Dominic was gentle and biddable but on occasions, infected with 'joie de vivre', used to gallop around the paddock, kicking up his heels. Once I was talking to my neighbour over the fence, when such a desire seized him. I was struck by his flailing hoofs as he galloped by, and had large bruises on my legs for several weeks. He was not, however, a 'kicker', and after a couple of experiences with the farrier, stood obediently to have his hoofs trimmed.

Dominic gradually acquired wives. The first, a very elderly jenny, was predictably called Jenny. She came to us a year or two after Dominic, and was thin and her coat was rough. With loving care, she regained her health. She became pregnant and produced a beautiful jenny whom I called Margarita. She was grey with a cross over her withers and down her back. The cross, according to legend, was a reminder that Christ had ridden this humble animal in triumph on Palm Sunday. There followed another three jennies. Donkeys were becoming popular, but very few were available from the domesticated population, so my three were transported from Western Queensland, captured from the so-called 'feral' population.

The first arrival I called Rosita. She had been handled briefly by the man who captured and transported her. I was anxious about how she would react to being relocated into the paddock. I was astounded when she allowed herself to be pushed from behind into the stable yard. There was no attempt to kick or resist. She must have been tired after the long trip, but her gentleness and acceptance were dominant qualities. She was a tall black donkey. Dominic and Margarita welcomed her and she soon settled.

Then came Fleur and Carlotta. Fleur was fawn in colour with a brown cross, while Carlotta was a rich brown without a cross.

Each of the jennies was fertile and produced a foal after eleven months. I tried to avoid getting too fond of the foals because I had decided to become a registered breeder and had to sell the foals when they were weaned. As a breeder and a committee member of the Donkey Society, I was expected to show donkeys at the Brisbane Exhibition, but had no success with Dominic.

I believed the jennies liked me to be present when they were about to give birth. It was invariably at night. They used to bray at the start of labour and I would go to encourage them. The word 'push, push' made the paddock sound like a labour ward. The labour was usually brief. When the foal had been cleaned by its mother, I picked it up and carried it to the closed stable with thick hay bedding so mother and baby could relax away from the curious eyes of the other donkeys. After a few days, when I was sure that the health of both was good, I let them out. Dominic and the jennies welcomed mother and baby and the other jennies were very gentle with the baby.

***

Margarita

Margarita was in labour. Usually labour lasts only a short time before the foal made its appearance, but this time she was in obvious distress so I called the vet. He used chains to pull the foal out. Unfortunately it was stuck because it had a frozen leg and could not have survived. Stitches for Margarita were required and I put her in the stable to give her lots of TLC. My own vet came to see because she would not eat or stand. It was Easter and he was going away. He said I must get her to stand. My wonderful neighbours came up every day, put a tarpaulin under her belly and held her up. She did not eat for a week but then quite suddenly ate some bread and then some oats. It was all good news from then on. Kim was so surprised – he thought we would lose her.

Apart from cream for her bedsores, she was soon up and about. Though I kept her away from Dominic for a year. Once they were together again, she soon produced a lovely foal. The death of the first foal (the only one I ever lost) and Margarita's illness upset me very much.

***

In the 1980s, Margarita was the cynosure of all eyes, when on three occasions she led the procession for the Palm Sunday service at the school where I taught, Somerville House. It was a special service for the boarders to which day pupils and parents were invited. In 1991 and 1992, I think, the service was held in the Assembly Hall. Margarita found the polished floor a challenge, since it was slippery, but she carried out her duties perfectly. The Chapel was opened in 1993. The aisle was carpeted, however she confidently stood for the whole service without urinating or defecating on the carpet, to my relief. I think she enjoyed the attention the girls gave her after her duties were done.

I lent Margarita several times for the Christmas manger situated in front of the Brisbane City Hall, where she was very popular. The human participants took turns but Margarita was on duty all the time and it went on for about a week. I supplied the food while others tended to her there. After 30 years with me, Margarita passed away in the late 1990s.

Because Gabriel, her last foal, so resembled Margarita, I decided to keep him. He had the same colouring with a cross but was much taller and had a fine conformation. I believe, had I been still showing donkeys, he would have won prizes. His temperament was gentle and affectionate. Unfortunately, I had him castrated because two entire jacks would have been unwise, however friendly they might have been to each other. In hindsight, perhaps I should have had Dominic castrated instead.

After the death of the four old jennies, who died at advanced ages, some estimated by the vets as in their thirties or even forties, I still had Gabriel.

To keep him company, I adopted a jennie called Ellie. Janine Dwyer, the equine vet, asked if I would adopt

Ellie after her owner was not able to care for her. Dominic had already died but his later years are chronicled in his relationship with Patch, the horse.

Ellie and Gabriel were good companions, when suddenly, Gabriel was affected with laminitis, a very painful inflammation of the lamina in the hoofs. One afternoon, I called him for his dinner, but he was in the back paddock, unable to stand. The vet, Janine, came and managed to transport him to the Redlands Equine Hospital. He was there for three weeks. I visited him every day. There was no improvement in spite of Janine's efforts. He would not eat and was very weak, so the decision was made to euthanise him. It was Christmas Eve of the year 2000 and I sat with him whispering comforting words until he slipped away. So Ellie was alone.

One day I noticed a pile of hedge cuttings which had been thrown over my fence from the neighbouring development. I threw them back onto the footpath, fearing they might be poisonous to Ellie. A man from a house in the development berated me, but I said that they were not my cuttings. The Brisbane City Council agreed to keep surveillance on my land. Someone (the same man? I do not know), threw palm fronds over my fence. Ellie chewed on them but could not digest them and she died. I was sad and very angry. I decided I would have no more donkeys, with unreliable neighbours in the developments on either side.

On a more cheerful note, before I leave the story of my donkeys, there are three incidents, two of which make me laugh whenever I think of them.

In the 1960s, there was a 'Top of the Pops' song called 'Dominique'. Every time that was played on the radio, Dominic rushed to the back door of the old house, braying. Since the song remained on the Hit Parade for several weeks, we had many noisy serenades from Dominic. He thought we were calling him.

A second incident occurred when Mum was in the house while the electrician dealt with my troublesome stove. Dominic, ever curious, decided to investigate that strange man, and entered the kitchen. Mum described how the electrician climbed onto the stove, shaking with terror, and remained there until Mum ushered Dominic out. How I wish I had seen the incident.

The third incident was painful for Mum at the time, but she soon saw the humorous side. Mum used to feed the animals when I was held up at the school with a meeting. She loved them but was also very strict with them, as she had been with me. She would not put feed in the trough until Patch the horse was tied up at his trough, and the donkeys had taken the places assigned to them. This was to avoid any unseemly jockeying for positions. Their evening meal consisted of pony pellets, bran, oats and lucerne chaff.

They were all eating contently, when Mum bent over to push Margarita's food into a pile. Margarita suddenly lifted her bony head and struck Mum in the eye. The next day, she went to my aunt's 90th birthday party, with a very black eye. When asked how she received the injury, Mum said, rather wryly, 'One of my grandchildren hit me.' She often used to say, because she had no human grandchildren, the animals filled that role. There were some very strange looks from those who did not know her, until she told the real story.

It was brought home to me one day how very seriously donkey owners were concerned about the reputation of their charges. I was on the committee of the Donkey Society. Two fellow members almost came to fisticuffs when disagreeing vehemently about whether it was degrading for the donkey to wear a hat. Members took sides with angry shouts. My calm view was that if the donkey was willing to accept that addition to his attire, then I did not object. I thought it was time to resign. Let's not anthropomorphise animals.

My donkeys were a constant source of pleasure to me and, I believe, they enjoyed their life at Winifred Street. There was heartache but there was much joy.

I think 'Nicholas Nye', a poem by Walter de la Mere, has two lines which sum up the character of donkeys and mine in particular.

'But a wonderful gumption was under his skin
And a clear, calm light in his eye.'

One Horse

"The wind of heaven is that which blows through a horse's ear."

Bedouin proverb

From a small child I had wanted a horse, so perhaps I should have introduced this with Shakespeare's words, spoken by Richard III, 'A horse, a horse, my kingdom for a horse'. Certainly, I would have given a kingdom, if I had one, for a horse.

My mother and father were both fine horse people. My father left school from his home at Teneriffe in Brisbane at the age fourteen to be a jackaroo on a property near Roma. He loved working with animals, but the drought in 1916 was so severe that he had to shoot dying animals. This upset him so much that he left the job and was apprenticed to a pattern maker. This trade was the most precise of all trades – making patterns in wood to be copied in metal. He lost his job in the Depression because he was young with no dependents. After the Depression he became a joiner and cabinet maker and I have a beautiful china cabinet that Dad made. Mum still had her job and she bought wood for him. They were engaged for eight years, because if they had married, there could have been a mother and father with possibly a baby living on the dole, which at that time required menial hard labour and a life of poverty for a family. They finally married in 1936, once my father had permanent work. I remained an only child.

My mother lived in Kin Kin, near Gympie. Her family moved there when she was twelve, after my grandfather became seriously ill with asthma, caused by the chemicals used in the tannery that he managed in Brisbane. This was the former tannery my dog Tony fell into years later. Mum loved the country life and the animals. Her horse Robin was a large grey of which she was very fond. She could also ride and manage Kaiser, a rather bad-tempered, flighty, sulky horse. When Nana was driving him, he invariably backed the sulky over the cliff beside the road, so Nana was left dangling. Nana hated country life; she was a Londoner. Mum had no trouble with Kaiser. He was named after Kaiser Wilhelm of Germany, who was extremely unpopular because he was blamed for causing World War I. Mum did not name him; he came with the property.

Like me, Mum loved horses and told the story of visiting the Royal Mews in London, with her class, while waiting to emigrate to Australia in 1912. She was nine. The royal horses were stabled at the Mews. Mum glimpsed a mother cat with kittens in a 'loose box' (a kind of food trough), that was also occupied by a very tall carriage horse. A horse and kittens! That was irresistible. Nothing daunted, she went in. Her teacher was horrified, fearing injury and was scolding her roundly, when two men in tweeds came on the scene. One asked her about her escapade. Mum told him about going to Australia and said confidently, "I am going to have a horse." The men moved on and the teacher was in a fluster, because the man who took such an interest was King George V with his vet. He and his vet were going to see a sick horse. It was unlikely that she would have had a horse as they were moving to Brisbane city. She knew better and Robin was her dream fulfilled.

It was inevitable that I should pester Mum and Dad for a horse. Quite rightly, they resisted my blandishments, because there was nowhere to keep a horse or to ride in many streets near busy Ipswich Road. I did not get a chance to fulfill my longing to ride until I was seven or eight, on our annual visit to Kin Kin in the August school holidays. Mum and I stayed with my mother's great friend from her Kin Kin days and Dad came to visit each weekend. I was in my element – horses, dogs, cattle, pigs and dairy cows aplenty.

On one early riding adventure, I was so proud one day to accompany Dad to ride into Kin Kin for supplies. My aunt had borrowed a neighbour's pony for me. Dad was on the farm's riding horse. All went well. We arrived at the farm gate. While Dad was opening it, the pony, sensing he was close to home, took off at a gallop. I clutched the meat I was carrying and his mane. I held on until there was a sharp turn on the track. Off I came, still clutching the meat and avoiding the barbed wire fence by a whisker. My Uncle Eddie, a very stern, frightening man, ordered me to get straight back into the saddle. I was shaken but not really hurt, so obeyed. Apparently, my uncle was right: the best remedy after a fall is to remount immediately. The fall did not deter me from riding again and I enjoyed that pastime each visit.

I did not welcome the longed-for horse until I was 30 years old. My near neighbour, a fine horsewoman herself, knew of my desire for a horse. She heard of a horse which was destined for the knackery and went to see that he was suitable for me.

No horse could have been more suitable, and she bought him for thirty pounds and rode him back to Kuraby from the opposite side of Brisbane. This was Apache, always called Patch. He was skewbald; brown and white and only eight years old. I could not believe that anyone could destroy such a beautiful horse just because he was no longer wanted.

We bonded immediately. He was gentle, reliable and very affectionate. My neighbour took me to buy a second-hand saddle and I was looking forward to riding in the bush with my neighbour. There was a hitch, however. When I put Patch into the paddock with Dominic, the donkey thought that Patch might have designs on his wives, so grabbed him by the neck and galloped poor Patch around the back paddock. Luckily, he was unhurt. I managed to separate them with great difficulty and kept them in adjoining paddocks until they started to make friends over the fence. I then put them together and from then on, they were very good affectionate friends.

To see them grooming each other by scratching each other's necks was a sign of real affection. Dominic, like all donkeys, hated water. In front of the house was a small dam that filled with water only when it rained, an unfortunate project of my then husband. On wet days, Patch used to get in and roll with great pleasure. Dominic was so worried about Patch's safety that he galloped around and around the dam, braying with anxiety. Dominic must have thought Patch was in danger, because *he* would never have entered the water of his own volition.

Patch and Dominic were allowed to graze together in the home paddock because they did not eat the garden plants. It was such a pleasure to see them close together grazing.

When my neighbour and I rode in the bush, Dominic liked to follow us. Patch was so reliable but once, when he was startled by a wallaby, he moved suddenly and I fell off. He stood completely still, gazed at me in some astonishment and waited patiently for me to remount.

Patch was particularly patient with children who had never ridden. I gave the mounted child the reins and walked beside the pair without leading Patch. I could trust him to follow me and the child thought he or she was riding 'properly'. When I had tired of walking with Patch, I would say to him, 'When you are ready, you shall have some bread.' Patch would move to the back door where the promised bread was produced, and he knew his job was done.

Patch was an example to all the donkeys when the farrier came. They really did not enjoy the experience, but Patch almost dozed off while his feet were trimmed.

A very amusing incident that I remember with pleasure occurred early one morning. Dominic and Patch were enjoying the lucerne on the lawn, when Dominic and I noticed simultaneously that someone had left the main gate open and there was a strange horse approaching the gate. Fearing a fracas, I set off as fast a pace as I could, to shut the gate and keep Patch away from the intruder. As I ran, the elastic in my skirt broke, so I arrived just in time to shut the gate, panting and clutching my descending skirt with one hand like a flamenco dancer. I do not think so, but hope that there were no early commuters to see my performance.

When Patch was thirty, I was overseas and the animals were being cared for by the daughters of Kim, my vet. Patch contracted colic, a very dangerous condition for horses. The girls called Kim immediately and he attended straight away. He could not, however, save him. As an equine specialist, Kim believed Patch probably had stomach cancer, as horses with grey or partly white patches do. Kim phoned me in Cyprus with the bad news. I must admit I was inconsolable for days. My Cyprus 'family' were so kind, but I had to go back to a home without Patch. This was, I think, in 1991. I realised how much Dominic was missing his mate. He spent much of his time in the house paddock looking quite lost.

I look back at my twenty-two happy years with Patch and Dominic with pleasure and some pain. Dominic lived for about two more years. One morning he was obviously in pain with bleeding from the anus. John, a neighbour, and I took him to the university equine hospital. They did not know what was amiss and sent Dominic home, only for him to die a few days later.

I then had a brief but happy visit by a miniature horse called Jules. She was agisted on my property and her company was enjoyed by the other animals and visiting friends.

The horses' and donkeys' stay with me for what seemed too short a time was a source of great joy.

"The horse, with beauty unsurpassed, strength immeasurable and grace unlike any other is still humble enough to carry a human on his back."
Amber Senti

"A pony is a childhood dream. A horse an adult treasure."
Rebecca Caroll

Appendix

PRIERE POUR ALLER AU PARADIS AVEC LES ANES

Lorsqu'il faudra aller vers vous, ô mon Dieu, faites que ce soit par un jour où la campagne en fête poudroiera. Je désire, ainsi que je fis ici-bas, choisir un chemin pour aller, comme il me plaira, au Paradis, où sont en plein jour les étoiles. Je prendrai mon bâton et sur la grande route j'irai, et je dirai aux ânes, mes amis : Je suis Francis Jammes et je vais au Paradis, car il n'y a pas d'enfer au pays du Bon Dieu. Je leur dirai : " Venez, doux amis du ciel bleu, pauvres bêtes chéries qui, d'un brusque mouvement d'oreille, chassez les mouches plates, les coups et les abeilles." Que je Vous apparaisse au milieu de ces bêtes que j'aime tant parce qu'elles baissent la tête doucement, et s'arrêtent en joignant leurs petits pieds d'une façon bien douce et qui vous fait pitié. J'arriverai suivi de leurs milliers d'oreilles, suivi de ceux qui portent au flanc des corbeilles,

de ceux traînant des voitures de saltimbanques
ou des voitures de plumeaux et de fer-blanc,
de ceux qui ont au dos des bidons bossués,
des ânesses pleines comme des outres, aux pas cassés,
de ceux à qui l'on met de petits pantalons
à cause des plaies bleues et suintantes que font
les mouches entêtées qui s'y groupent en ronds.
Mon Dieu, faites qu'avec ces ânes je Vous vienne.
Faites que, dans la paix, des anges nous conduisent
vers des ruisseaux touffus où tremblent des cerises
lisses comme la chair qui rit des jeunes filles,
et faites que, penché dans ce séjour des âmes,
sur vos divines eaux, je sois pareil aux ânes
qui mireront leur humble et douce pauvreté
à la limpidité de l'amour éternel.

Frances Jammes
Source: https://www.poesie.net/jam1.htm

TRANSLATION OF 'PRIÈRE POUR ALLER AU PARADIS AVEC LES ÂNES'

PRAYER TO GO TO HEAVEN WITH THE DONKEYS

When I have to join you, O Lord, let it be
on one of those days when the joyful countryside sparkles.
I wish to choose, as I did down below,
a path of my liking to reach paradise,
where stars shine bright in broad daylight.
I will take my staff and, on the high road,
I will say to the donkeys, my friends:
"I am Francis Jammes on my way to paradise,

for there is no hell in the land of our good Lord."
I will tell them, "Come, sweet friends of the blue sky,
poor dear beasts who chase off with your lively ears
flies, blows and bees alike".
May I meet You among these beasts, O Lord,
for I love them so, as they gently
bow their heads and stop, joining their tiny feet
in a meek manner that arouses Your mercy.
I will come, followed by their thousand ears,
by those who bear baskets on their flanks,
those who pull acrobat carts,
or carts full of a tinker's gear,
those who bear on their backs big dented cans,
the jennies with their swollen bellies and broken step,'
those who are given small trousers
to protect them from the blue seeping wounds
that droves of stubborn flies inflict on them.
O Lord, let me come to You among those donkeys.
Let angels lead us in peace
toward swollen streams reflecting cherries
smooth as the laughing flesh of young girls,
and let me be, in this resting place of the souls,
as I lean over Your divine waters, like the donkeys,
who will mirror their humble and gentle poverty
in the clear pool of eternal love.

Translation by Barbara Merefield
Source: http:lyricstranslate.com

Jenny the jenny, with her newly born foal Margarita

Breakfast time – Dominic the donkey, Patch the horse and the girls (jennies), with Sheba the dog overseeing

Margarita and her foal – "I'm OK Mum."

Margarita's moment of triumph – Palm Sunday Service Somerville House, 1995

Rosita, Carlotta and Fleur grazing in the paddock at Kuraby

Fleur, with a cross on her back

Dominic grazing in the paddock

Dominic the jack donkey, with his fly veil

Unnamed foal, probably Rosita's. I tried (not very successfully) not to get too close as a newborn

Pamela's mother on her horse Robin, a large grey

Pamela's dearly loved horse Patch (Apache), with his skewbald patches

Jules the miniature horse with a visiting friend and Pamela

Chapter 4
Three Sows and a Boar

"No pig can fly, but they are capable of far more amazing things."
Claire Wilkinson (my cousin)

I first became enamoured of pigs when holidaying at the farm in Kin Kin as a child. The pigs there were pink and friendly, though hardly pets. They did, however, have a large outdoor yard and a 'rolly-hole'. It was explained that pigs have no sweat glands and to keep cool, a water-filled mud wallow is essential. Because of their mud-encrusted bodies, pigs have a reputation for being dirty. On the contrary, they are scrupulously clean. They urinate and defecate well away from their eating and sleeping areas, and their sleeping areas never need attention apart from sweeping.

Now, having seen pigs confined in small spaces, I understand how it must pain them to be forced to change their natural, evolved behaviour. They are extremely intelligent, as my adventures with Penelope, Portia, Pandora and Oliver, will, I hope, show.

I cannot remember now why Mum and I visited the Ipswich Show in about 1980. Perhaps it was something to do with donkeys. Imagine my excitement (and my mother's too I am sure), when over in the animal nursery there was a sow with a litter of piglets. Mother and babies were all black. Mother pig was not very large and the piglets were ready to be weaned. I chose an alert looking female. She slept on the back seat of the car all the way home. I had already decided to call her Penelope, after the faithful wife of Ulysses in 'Homer's Odyssey'.

Because there was no pen ready for her, I decided to keep her in the house until her home was prepared. During the day, she stayed in the kitchen and at night, on a small trampoline bed in the quite large toilet. Knowing the clean habits of pigs, I waited to see where she would urinate, washed the floor with Dettol and spread thick newspaper there. As I expected, I never had to clean elsewhere. She was gentle and affectionate and the dogs and cats accepted her. Both Mum and I loved her.

After about a fortnight, her new quarters were ready; a long, fairly narrow shed which had been used by former owners as an orchid house. Penelope moved in. One end, the furthest from the gate, she quickly established as the place to toilet; half way along was her rolly-hole; and closest to the door was her eating and sleeping area.

She enjoyed joining Mum weeding outside her pen when she was very young. She snuffled about in the grass and, one suspects, removed the occasional plant.

Penelope enjoyed her food, as most pigs do. I thought she still needed milk, reasoning she must miss her mother's milk. The produce agent produced a milk powder which they told me was suitable for recently weaned pigs. That did not attract her, so for the rest of her life, I added raspberry cordial to the milk. She loved that and also enjoyed pig pellets, a variety of fruit and vegetables as well as grass. There was an occasional treat of jelly beans and bread.

Once she was rather lethargic and not eating with her usual gusto, so I called my wonderful vet, Kim Smith. I have a memory which makes me smile whenever I think of it. It is of Kim lying full-length near the gate, taking her temperature, his face in the straw. Penelope was very amenable; the job was accomplished, bronchitis diagnosed and suitable antibiotics administered, first by injection and then followed up inside peanut butter sandwiches. Most of my large animals loved that treat and I usually tried to get them 'hooked' on that combination. They consumed it enthusiastically when needing medication for an illness, which could be administered on the sandwich.

One Christmas Eve, I must have left the door of the pen unlatched and Penelope went off exploring. I was frantic with anxiety and drove around the neighbourhood calling her name. One of my more distant neighbours was out watering his garden and did not know of my menagerie. He enquired anxiously whether I had lost a child. When I replied, 'No, my pig,' he looked at me very oddly.

Not far from my home there is a school, which was not fenced. Calling for Penelope, I heard sounds of excited grunting, and she appeared. I wondered how I was to get her home. Not optimistically, I opened the car door and without hesitation, she jumped in and sat on the front seat. She looked so regal, I expected a royal wave. She rode home and then followed me into her pen with, I suspect, some relief.

Penelope's pen had been rebuilt since her earlier home and was larger and airier, with more access to natural shade. She appeared to be very happy there because she could see all the activity around her – the other animals, my movements, the mower man and Mum, when she was gardening nearby.

When Penelope was about seven years old, she became ill and would not eat her food but would nibble only on grass I pulled for her. I phoned the university pig facility at Brookfield and Dr Ranald Cameron sent a float to collect her. Dr Cameron, now long retired and with whom I am still in touch, was wonderful. He tried every possible test. The girls there loved Penelope because they usually dealt with commercial pigs, whereas Penelope was interactive, affectionate and a pet.

After several weeks, during which I visited most days, she appeared to improve. Dr Cameron thought she was missing me too much, so he allowed her to return home. Soon, however, her health deteriorated and she returned to the hospital. Dr Cameron rang me at school to say she was terminally ill and asked my permission to euthanise her. He also asked if he could do an autopsy, to which I was willing to agree, if other pigs could be helped. The result indicated that she had cancer of the uterus, a condition which seems to occur in sows that have never had a litter. This is rare, as few breeding sows live to a mature age without having offspring, while the young are usually slaughtered for the meat market. I had loved Penelope so much, that I mourned for ages, as did Mum. She was a friend. Of all the thousands of pigs Dr Cameron treated, he still remembers Penelope.

Having experienced the joy of pig ownership, I was happy to adopt a little wild pig whose mother had been shot. She was black with white spots on her rump, like an appaloosa horse. I called her Portia, a particularly apposite name.

There was a prominent Roman family called Porcius, the best known of whom was Marcus Porcius Cato. Porcius means 'pig' in Latin. How the family acquired such a strange name is a mystery. Cato's daughter was Portia, (often spelt 'Porcia'). She was the devoted wife of Brutus, one of the assassins of Julius Caesar. On her husband's death, she committed suicide by swallowing fire.

My Portia developed into an affectionate pet, though she lacked the charisma and intelligence of Penelope. I did ask Dr Cameron if she ought to be spayed, but he advised against it, saying it was a very long operation. Sadly, she also succumbed to uterine cancer at about six years old.

My next pig, also the offspring of a wild sow which had been shot, was black. Like Portia, Pandora was affectionate, gentle and amenable.

I called her Pandora, in keeping with the classical theme. Her namesake had opened the box which released all the woes into the world. Only Hope remained.

The bush next door was being cleared for development. When I saw prospective buyers looking at a block next to my fence, I spoke to them, pointing out that I had animals and if they had any concerns, they could contact me. Instead, they approached my local alderman, demanding I get rid of the rooster, the goats the sheep and the pig. The rooster was illegal in a closely settled neighbourhood, so I found a home for him on a friend's farm. Fortunately, the alderman said, 'You were here first, but can you move the pig to a different location on the property?'

The foreman, Guy Beresford, who was managing the development, was very kind to me and we are still in touch. My wonderful neighbour of fifty years, John Turner, built a new 'deluxe' pen with a raised sleeping and eating area, entered via a ramp, with a large shaded run and a rolly-hole at the far end. A tyre was suspended on a chain to keep Pandora occupied, as well as some large plastic balls to push around the pen.

The foreman, Guy, made a passage using the large orange plastic netting used by Police and builders, to lead her safely to her new home. Initially she was rather depressed but soon settled in with the aid of jelly beans and lots of TLC. Pandora lived several years in her new pen.

Pandora was thirteen, a good age for a pig, when she died suddenly, probably from a heart attack. I missed her but she had a happy fulfilled life with her playthings, settled amongst the other animals.

After the death of Pandora, I had almost decided to have no more pigs, their loss was so powerful.

Fate, however, intervened. In about 2008, my cousin Claire, herself an animal lover, phoned with an offer I could not refuse. She lives in Goomeri, a country town about 300km north of Brisbane. A neighbour had asked if she knew of anyone who could adopt a pig. Apparently, she had bought a male pig purporting to be a miniature. Her dog was harassing him.

Claire immediately phoned me and, as she and her husband were driving to see me, they brought Oliver down, sleeping peacefully on the back seat of their car. I would have called him Patrick but did not want to confuse him by changing his name. The original owner was told by the breeder that he would grow no higher than her knee. Well, unless my knee is at my waist, the breeder was guilty of false advertising. I told her so, and she finally admitted she had bred down from runts. This made him vulnerable to all sorts of illnesses.

When Oliver was still quite young, he became very ill and went to the Manly Road vet hospital, where he underwent an eight-hour operation for an obstruction of his gut. The vet, one of my former students, worked tirelessly and he recovered. When I asked her how she managed to stand so long, she replied, 'They fed me Mars Bars.' I needed more than Mars Bars to recover from the bill, even though it was discounted.

Later in his life, Oliver suffered from pneumonia. This time it was off to Dayboro, where the university hospital was newly situated. There he was successfully treated and recovered well.

Other visits followed for more mundane procedures such as hoof trimming. Oliver was less amenable than the girls to this indignity and had to be sedated with twenty-four Valium. He slept like a baby and woke suddenly with no sign of a 'hangover'. His feed was similar to that of the girls but I cooked his vegetables – sweet potato, potato, carrot, brussels sprouts, turnips and more – because the vet felt that cooking his vegetables would help his gut to avoid another blockage. He also had fruit, pig pellets and raspberry milk – a good balanced diet, though rather expensive!!

Second only to food, he loved to have his tummy scratched when he was either lying down or standing. He indicated his pleasure by grunting loudly and marking time with his feet. He was so large that he intimidated John Turner when he was carrying out repairs to his pen, so Valium was employed with the same successful results as with his hoof-trimming procedure. In spite of his size and his masculinity, Oliver never attempted to bite, though he appeared to prefer women to men. Although castrated, Oliver had tusks like a hog, but they were filed periodically.

A year ago, when he was almost fifteen years old, I became housebound which made it impossible to care for the big animals – three sheep, a goat and Oliver. I had faithful friends who fed them and then rushed off to work or school, so the animals lacked human interaction. It was no life for them.

When a friend and a former student, Trish and her husband Doug, offered to rehome them, at Eerwah Vale, in the Sunshine Coast Hinterland, I thought it was a happy solution. They were taken to their new home by an animal transporter in a float carefully divided to accommodate each species. I worried about how Oliver would travel – he was so old. Dr Cameron said he had never heard of a fifteen-year-old pig. All was well. After only a few weeks in their new home, I was invited to visit for the weekend. The setting was glorious, lots of birds, beautiful gardens and an abundance of wildlife. It had been a former dog breeder's home; there were pens for each of them and a large grazing area. When I called their names, Oliver and the goat came to greet me. Oliver stood beside me so I could scratch his tummy and the goat was equally enthusiastic. The sheep were more 'standoffish', and I am so grateful to Trish and Doug for their devoted care. The animals have already formed a bond with their new owners, who keep me up to date with anecdotes of the animals' new lives at Eerwah Vale.

Although Oliver spent a relatively short time with Trish and Doug, I asked if they would write an account of his life after he left me. I am including it here because it is so insightful and a tribute to the kindness of Trish and Doug and Oliver's adaptability and *his* genuine love for *his* humans.

Oliver
By Trish

It was with great excitement but some nervousness that we welcomed Bacchus, the goat and Jason, Medea and Festus, the sheep and Oliver, the pig to their new home. Sheep did not seem much of a challenge but we had heard horror stories about caring for goats and that pig, Oliver, was so huge!

Minutes after a very orderly arrival, all animals were settled in their pens. Oliver, in particular, enjoyed a splash in his water trough, grunting in delight as he nudged the cold water over himself, sending cascades over the sides.

The animals arrived with Pamela's instructions on how to feed them. I followed these to the letter, doling out exactly the number of slices of carrots, apple, sweet potato and scoops of pellets that were written down. This was out of respect for Pamela who had loved and cared for these five for many years. Now, in her eighties, she needed someone else to care for them to the same high standard.

How Oliver loved his food!

He also proved to be very chatty. He loved to grunt as he lumbered towards you for a pat or, even better, a good scratch. A few days after he arrived, we let him out to free range with his companions, confident that, with food to tempt him, he would be easy to direct back into his pen.

On his second day out, I sat in a camp chair in the paddock in order for the animals to get to know me. I was talking to my daughter over the fence when Oliver approached for a chat. He snorted and grunted as his massive, black body headed towards me. The noise was very loud.

Holly tentatively said, "Mum, how do you know he's being friendly?"

I suddenly realised my vulnerability. Sitting low, there was no way I could get out of his way if that snorting was not a sign of friendship!

There was no need to worry. Doug and I would subsequently have many chats with Oliver as he relished his days in the sun, wandering round the paddock, clearly the alpha animal of this motley crew. We had to make sure the gates to the pens of Bacchus and the sheep were locked each morning or we would always find Oliver snoozing in one of their pens, causing much indignation to the rightful owners.

We were delighted when Pamela visited us after a month so she could see her dearly loved animals in their new environment. One afternoon, as we sat on the wooden bench next to the fence, Oliver headed over for a catch-up. I am sure he heard her ask me if he had made a 'rolly-hole' yet. He had not, at that point, but within a few days, Doug began renovations in his pen. From then on, it was difficult to keep his water trough full. Each day, the rolly-hole grew larger as he tipped his trough over and then proceeded to wallow. He was as happy as a pig in mud!!

Eventually we could see his trotters needed attention – or, as I would say, "You need your toe nails cut, Oliver." The hunt was on for someone to do them. Pamela talked to the vet who used to do them but he lived too far away; we approached the vet who used to tend our cows but his practice did not offer pig toenail services; eventually, our daughter, Eliza, through her contacts, traced down a vet who did pig work. Oliver would need to be sedated, so a few days before the procedure, I collected 80 tablets that needed to be fed to him an hour before the vet was due. The theory was that he would be sleeping, the trotters would be clipped as he slept and Bob's your uncle – no worries.

When the day arrived, I duly took his breakfast up to him, hidden in which were the 80 tablets. He got an extra peanut butter sandwich that morning! I left him snuffling up the breakfast fare, thinking how easy this was proving to be. We heard the vet arrive and guided him up past the house to where the animal pens and paddock were. Much to everyone's surprise, there was Oliver, standing at his gate, a little groggy but still full of life.

We should have realised it would not go at all well when this vet exclaimed, "He's huge! I usually work with little pigs, putting in nose rings. Has he ever had a go at you?"

It was clear that Oliver needed further sedation but the vet seemed too scared to enter the pen. I offered to make some more peanut butter sandwiches while Doug offered to inject him if the vet was happy to give Doug the needle – he was. Oliver certainly had a great constitution for a fifteen-year-old pig. Eventually, Oliver did slump to the ground but when the vet tried to cut through his trotter, he still had the strength to raise his head and attempt to bite. The job was done with Doug lying across Oliver's body holding down his head.

It was obvious to us the next day that the vet had done a poor job, as Oliver hobbled on a bloodied foot. Not unexpectedly, the vet would not answer our calls. Oliver was most upset with Doug who needed to be very nimble on his feet if entering the pen. Oliver had a go at him a few times, rushing at him and squealing – quite disconcerting, having such a huge animal thundering towards you with malice in this heart!

After this, Oliver's health deteriorated. Some mornings he would not want his breakfast, so we knew he was off colour. He stopped coming out of his pen, spending hours sleeping. We wondered if the sedation had been too much for him. Pamela consulted two vets who had known Oliver for many years and we called our vet who was happy to treat him. Between the vets, Oliver was diagnosed as having an adverse reaction to his long-term pain medication and infected tusks. At this point, the vet talked about his age and the possibility that he was nearing the end of his life. However, his medication was changed and he went on antibiotics for the infection.

Talk about Lazarus! Before long, he was eating and wandering short distances outside his pen. He decided to make a new rolly-hole right next to the main water trough in the paddock. He tipped the water out of it and made a huge muddy puddle right next to it. The other animals were not at all impressed. Presumably, because it was a further distance to walk to his rolly-hole, Oliver made a new home for himself in the closest pen to the water trough. We put in hay for sleeping and a solid concrete trough for his drinking water and decided to just go with his wishes. By this time, he had forgiven Doug. It was Doug who helped him to his feet those mornings that were just too tough on the old bones. Oliver would talk to Doug a lot, always wandering over to say hello if he was about.

Oliver did get to leave a permanent reminder on Doug. During this period of ill health, we had to give him some antibiotic treatment. Doug once again had to inject him, never an easy task. We had him pushed into the corner of the pen as Doug forced the needle in. Oliver swung round to see what was going on and one of his tusks caught Doug's leg, tearing a long but shallow strip down his leg. A trip to the emergency department of the local hospital, a thorough clean and antibiotics ensured all was well. Oliver seemed particularly attentive to Doug after this. Was he really saying "sorry", as Doug insists, or is that all wishful thinking?

That last month was quite a roller coaster of emotions for everyone as Oliver's health waxed and waned. Just when we thought his last days were near, he would come alive and be standing in his pen, ready and eager for his food. Eventually though, he couldn't get up. We put up a cover over his rolly-hole, where he lay, to protect him from the intense heat and called the vet again. The diagnosis this time was a bad sprain, or perhaps, a broken bone in his leg. There was more medication to see if he would pick up but also the chat about his age and nearing end of life. Pamela was talking to his old vet and we all dreaded having to make a call to end his life.

That night, we made him as comfortable as we could in his rolly-hole, knowing it would be too painful for him to get to his feet and move back to his pen. We thought that tomorrow we would all have to make a decision about what was best for him.

At dawn the next morning, we rose, not wanting to face the day. Imagine our amazement as we looked out on the paddock to see Oliver, standing just beyond the fence, nearest the house. He had travelled at least 40 metres overnight! With great urging from Doug, we were able to get him to walk back to his pen. We left him there to await a call from the vet and further discussion with Pamela.

I went to check on him as the heat of the day intensified. There he was, the old fellow who had battled so hard, finally at rest. My first thought was, "He took the decision out of our hands. Thank you, Oliver."

This wonderful old pig who gave us so much pleasure in the last six months of his life, is buried in a quiet, shady spot under Mt Eerwah. Like all amazing animals we have been privileged to know, he lives on in our memories.

The following quotation is from Charlotte's Web, the famous children's story about a friendship between a spider and a pig. It reflects the daily life and affection of my animal friends, particularly Oliver, who I always thought was 'hatching' something.

> *"Life is always a rich and steady time when you are waiting for something to happen or to hatch."*
> E.B. White

Penelope the pig in conversation with Pamela

Penelope in her winter coat –
"Surely the grass is greener on the other side."

Pandora looking content in her pen

Pandora in her rolly-hole – "Oh the bliss"

Oliver, who never attempted to bite, with his healthy treats

The affectionate Portia –
Is it dinnertime yet

Oliver in Eewah Vale. He lived
to the good age of 15

Chapter 5

Sheep to the Right, Goats to the Left

The Sheep

"The shepherd always tries to persuade the sheep that their interests and his own are the same."
Stendhal

I have many happy memories of the sheep in my life, though I must, however, admit that my shepherding did not always agree with their interests.

My first sheep arrived one day in a red sportscar driven by a trainee vet, who was accompanied by one of my former students, his girlfriend. She nursed a tiny lamb. Apparently, the young man was doing his work experience at the abattoirs. One of the ewes gave birth to the lamb and the mother was immediately slaughtered. I was horrified. She suffered the pain of giving birth but could not even see her baby. I, of course, agreed to adopt Agnes, named from the Greek for 'chaste' but often used for 'lamb', as in Agnes Dei. I always called her Ness. I used to feed her three times during the night and each morning on my way to school, I took her to Mum to do the day shift.

Agnes developed scours (diarrhoea) on cow's milk. The vet advised boiled water until suitable milk powder could be purchased. She recovered and returned to the routine of six meals a day until she was old enough to nibble grass and lucerne. She still had a bottle at bedtime!

Because Agnes never knew her mother, I became her

substitute. We were still living in the old house, where the bathroom was beside the back door. One night I was in the bath and Agnes came bouncing in and jumped into the bath. We were both rather surprised!

I used to leave my school carry bag beside the back door, where it was easy to collect on my way to the car. Agnes found it one day, and chewed the contents – the students' essays, which I had finished correcting the night before. It was not a case of, 'the dog ate my homework', but rather, 'the lamb ate your homework'. The girls took it in good part, I am glad to say. They loved to hear stories of my animals.

Agnes continued to be my shadow for many years, though she was joined about a year later by another orphaned lamb, rescued from a sheep station out west by a friend. The new female lamb was so pretty – mostly black, but with brown legs, face and tail, and a little flash of white on her face and the tip of her tail. I could not bear to have her continuously waving tail removed, so I always had to be vigilant about fly-strike.

One of my mother's favourite expressions was, 'I will be with you in two shakes of a lamb's tail', meaning very soon. In England, where Mum was born, and where lamb's tails were not removed, people knew first-hand how quickly lambs shook their tails. In Australia, one rarely saw a lamb with a tail. Fly-strike, if neglected, is fatal.

I called this delightful little creature Madelaine. She and Agnes were good friends and companions, and both lived to be quite old. I had them shorn each Spring by an eighty-year-old retired shearer. He was so careful that he never once cut them.

When he finally retired, I found another shearer who was much more slapdash. He cut Agnes, and although I treated the wound, she died of tetanus. I did not even have time to call the vet. Madelaine lived for a short time longer but died suddenly, probably from a heart attack. They were each about thirteen.

While I still had the two much loved sheep, I adopted an entire ram. The vet's daughter was moving from a hobby farm to the suburbs. He was already called Bunter – his name should have made me suspicious about his character. Bunter was certainly affectionate and loved to have his head rubbed around his horns. One day I was digging a ditch in his paddock when Bunter came up to be petted. I complied for a time then told him I was busy so he must go away.

I recovered my spade and resumed digging. Bunter, who did not appreciate his neglect, 'bunted' me so hard that I fell face-first into the mud in the ditch. Only my pride was hurt, but I was careful not to turn my back on him again.

Bunter fell in love with my curly-coated retriever Charlotte. He lay as close to the fence of his paddock as he could, and Charlotte, seemingly returning his affection, lay right next to the fence on the other side and they lay there for hours on end. It was an interesting close friendship. Bunter lived for many years and died peacefully of old age. In spite of his eccentricities, I missed Bunter when he died.

It was several years before I acquired more sheep. A friend had two sheep agisted on my property. I used to feed them. I became fond of them but they were not mine. The father of the girl who owned them said she had too many animals and she was either to sell them or give them to me. I was happy to adopt them both and named them Jason and Medea since they had been unnamed.

In Greek mythology, Jason was helped in his search for the Golden Fleece by a sorceress, Medea, and when he found it, the pair fled together. They presumably lived happily for many years with their two sons, one of whom was Festes. Jason, however, tired of her, and in revenge, Medea murdered the boys and was carried to safety in a chariot by a god. She was obviously a thoroughly unpleasant person. There was no end to her nastiness and neither Jason nor Medea was an admirable character. Jason died when a plank from the 'Argo' fell on him while he slept beside the ship.

There is another, even more disturbing story, to be found in the works of a Greek playwright of the fourth century BC, Euripides. The play is called simply, 'Medea'. Euripides wrote several plays about mythical women, with a degree of empathy towards women not found in many males in the Greek world.

Euripides' version tells how Jason and Medea lived in Corinth, ruled by King Cleon. Jason, perhaps wishing to advance himself, abandoned Medea to marry the king's daughter. Medea was a sorceress and vowed revenge.

She sent her sons with a gift for the new bride. When the girl donned the beautiful robe, she was engulfed by fire. When Cleon rushed to help his daughter, he too was incinerated. After the vengeful Medea had murdered her sons, she fled with the aid of a god driving a chariot through the sky. Later, Medea found refuge with King Aegeus.

Medea contemplating the murder of her boys, depicting the anxious tutor behind - Wall painting from Ancient Pompeii (Source: ancient-origins.net)

I called my two sheep Jason and Medea after these mythological figures and they had a son, whom I called Festes. To avoid friction between them, I had both Jason and Festes castrated and they lived happily with me until they joined Oliver and the goat at

Eewah Vale. Because they were 'a flock' I became less close to them than I was to Agnes, Madelaine and Bunter. Trish has provided a tale about Jason, Medea and Festes.

Jason, Medea and Festes
By Trish

I sometimes feel sorry for the sheep, living their lives in the shadow of the big personalities of Oliver, the large black pig and Bacchus, the delightfully bossy goat.

Jason, with his black head and cape and his misshapen ear, is the steady hand at the head of his family; Medea, the creamy white, gentle Mum; and Festes, the black headed adolescent, full of inquisitiveness, bravado and sense of entitlement. Medea still grooms her boy while Jason watches over them both.

The sheep are shy and tentative characters, particularly Medea who always defers to Jason and Festes around mealtimes. I have spoken to her about feminism but so far she is not listening.

Festes has a fair-weather friend in Bacchus. They can often be seen jousting, head to head. It is obviously only a game though, because when Bacchus seriously takes charge, Festes does not stand a chance. He is put firmly in his place.

The sheep are relaxed and happy spending their days grazing the paddock or sitting together in the shade on a hot day. They begrudgingly allow Bacchus to be part of their herd, although they probably don't get a lot of say in that.

The sheep demonstrate a lot of love and care for each other which is humbling to watch. Animals can teach us a lot about those qualities that we call humanity.

The Goats

"It is good for a person to be terrorised by a goat. It is difficult to be high and mighty when there's something chasing you for vegetables."
                                                Sasha Pulley

I can never understand why goats, in Biblical times, were regarded as outcasts. Jesus, in Matthew 25, will draft off the sheep to his right and the goats to his left. The sheep, he said, were the righteous, and the goats, the rebel non-believers.

There are many references to goats in the Old Testament, few of them with approval. The practice with the 'scapegoat' has already been mentioned in Chapter 3. The goat must have been very important to the farming economy yet they are so often deprecated. Is it because goats produced only milk and meat and not wool? Admittedly there is something rather sinister about a goat's eyes, with the rectangular iris. Once I owned goats, this initial reaction was belied.

My cousin Winifred gave me my first kid. This kid was white and delightful and was one of the procession of animals led by Dante who went off exploring. I called her Polly. She lived for many years amicably with Jason and Madelaine. After Polly's death I was without goats for several years.

I eventually adopted two adult castrated goats. I called them Dionysus and Ulysses.

The God of wine in Greek mythology was Dionysus. His sacred animal was the goat, supposedly because the goat was known for his liking for the leaves of the grapevine. This would seem to be counterproductive, but who can account for the reasoning of the ancients?

Dionysus was a little white domestic goat. His companion Ulysses was named after the Greek warrior who sailed from Troy and finally arrived 10 years later at his home in Ithaca, to be greeted by his loyal wife Penelope. Ulysses the goat was brown with floppy ears and alert expression.

Dionysus had fairly moderate horns which he used to get caught in the wire which separated his pen from that of Ulysses. Helen and I were constantly struggling to wrestle him free. I doubt it was from a desire for Ulysses' company. He probably thought the lucerne, pellets and vegetables looked better 'on the other side'.

Like all goats, they loved their food. My friend Helen looked after my animals on several occasions when I was overseas. She wrote amusingly of their antics.

The Goats
By Helen

Having made the acquaintance of Dionysus and Ulysses, I came to the conclusion that goats keep their brains in their horns. Dionysus had horns and obviously did a bit of thinking. You could look into his eyes and see that something was going on inside. He wasn't malicious or devious, but seemed to be weighing me up. His horns were a bit of a problem at times, because he would somehow get them caught between the slats of his sleeping platform and I would have to wrestle his head around to get him out. Ulysses had no horns and was totally brainless. He reminded me of one of the strange creatures in Star Wars; brown, lanky, with floppy ears and enthusiastically helpful, but unfailingly clumsy.

At feeding time, the two would line up at the fence and wait for me to throw some lucerne hay over. Dionysus, being the bossier of the two, would get his hay first and immediately tuck in, positioning himself in such a way that Ulysses couldn't join him. Then I would move along the fence a little way, and make sure that Ulysses was watching before throwing the hay more or less in front of him. He would then look up at the sky and turn his head this way and that, looking for his flying hay. He was definitely the last person you would want for your basketball team. Dionysus was well aware of Ulysses' directional problem, and at this point, while Ulysses was performing his inelegant pirouettes, would leave his own feed and amble slyly along the fence to eat Ulysses' feed. Ulysses just got the leftovers.

One afternoon, Helen went to feed them and found Dionysus dead in the paddock, probably from a heart attack or a stroke. Both goats were gentle and quite old. Ulysses lived a little longer but died from old age and probably because he missed his friend. I was very sad – they had been pleasant, companionable (and always hungry) pets.

My last two goats were Bacchus and Ariadne. Their names were also derived from Greek/Roman mythology. Bacchus was the Roman name for Dionysus and Ariadne was his great human love. Their story is an interesting one. In far off times, Greece was required to send a sacrificial group of seven young men and seven young maidens to the Minotaur, a half-human and half-bull monster, who lived in the labyrinth in the palace of Minos in Crete.

Theseus, son of Aegeus, the ruler of Attica, offered to join the group in order to kill the Minotaur. Theseus met Ariadne, daughter of Minos of Crete, and he fell in love. I find it strange that people destined to be sacrificed should meet socially with the 'sacrificers'. Ariadne helped Theseus by providing him with a sword and a ball of string, to help him find his way out of the maze.

The Minotaur slain, Theseus and Ariadne fled with her brother. Minos pursued them, furious that the Minotaur was killed. His ship was gaining on that of Theseus, so Ariadne's brother was killed and his body cut up, and the portions thrown overboard. Minos had to collect the body parts in order to give his son a proper burial.

The fugitives escaped to Naxos, a small island off Greece. Theseus, however, had a very bad memory, and left Ariadne behind on Naxos, while he sailed home to Greece.

Once again, his memory failed him, very conveniently it seems. He had promised his elderly father, Aegeus, the ruler of Attica, that if the expedition had been successful, the sail would be white; if unsuccessful, the sail would be black. Either he 'forgot' to change the sail, or ran a black one up by mistake, but the king saw the black sail and, in despair, threw himself from a cliff into the sea and died. This is how the Aegean Sea was named.

Theseus became king. Meanwhile, Dionysus (Bacchus) found the sleeping Ariadne on the island of Naxos; they fell in love and he made her a star in the sky, where she remains today. Hence, the goats' names – Bacchus and Ariadne.

Bacchus and Ariadne proved to be 'characters', like their namesake gods. Ariadne was a rich chocolate brown in colour with limpid, friendly brown eyes. She was devoted to Dionysus, who sometimes was not kind to her, bunting to get to his pen and food first.

Bacchus was an Eastern type of goat, very common in Syria, Lebanon and Cyprus. He was dark brown with black and white patches and very long curving horns, which he was not averse to using on me if I was a little slow in doing what he wanted. He was an expert escapee, but fortunately Ariadne did not follow him.

One day, I had an agitated phone call from a neighbour. Bacchus was grazing in his back yard, having manoeuvred his horns through a single fence paling. His body had followed. I immediately collected a bowl of food, phoned Dennis who used to do 'handyman' jobs, and went up to call Bacchus, who came immediately when I shook the food bowl. I sat down across the opening so he could not return to his illicit grazing. When I tried to get up, I was unable to do so, even with the aid of my walking stick. I might still have been there, if Dennis had not come quickly to mend the fence. He rescued me and herded Dionysus into his pen with more food and all was well. At least I had not been bunted this time, like my experience with Bunter the sheep.

Ariadne was a gentle girl and always looked rather hurt when Bacchus bunted her. He was fond of her, I am sure, but food came first.

When they were both quite old, I noticed Ariadne was often leaving some of her food. I also noticed she was reluctant to sit down. I thought she had arthritis and gave her Bute, an anti-inflammatory drug. I also gave her lots of soft food: grapes and other soft fruit and vegetables as well as peanut butter sandwiches with the Bute. I realised how thin she was becoming and called the vet, who diagnosed arthritis of the jaw, apparently not uncommon in goats. There was nothing to be done. In about 2019, I had to make the painful decision to euthanise her. It broke my heart – she was such a gentle creature.

Bacchus seemed to miss her but continued his escaping ways. When the animals went with Trish and Doug to Eewah Vale a few months ago, he was among them. Apparently, he enjoys the company of the sheep there, but is still escaping. Doug, however, only has to call him and he returns. Is there something Doug is not telling me? Is there a treat to bring him back? Bacchus certainly seemed pleased to see me when I visited, and came for a pat when I called him. Trish shared this story of Bacchus.

Bacchus the Goat
By Trish

I first met Bacchus at Pamela's house. I chatted to him through the fence before wandering off to visit the sheep and pig, located elsewhere.

Returning to the house, I felt a presence; the feeling you get when someone is staring at you. Sure enough, up on a nearby hillock stood Bacchus, observing everything that was going on – a portent for things to come.

Not long after he and his mates came to live with us, he earned the nickname, 'The Supervisor'. Nothing happens in the paddock that Bacchus now shares with the motley crew that he does not supervise. Whether we are tending to the pig, doling out the food or cleaning the pens, Bacchus always takes a keen interest. He sometimes lends a hand, bunting the sheep from their pen if we are working there. He isn't above trying to gobble down their feed either, if we let him.

His supervisory duties extend beyond his own paddock. Numerous times as we entertain guests on our back veranda, we discover that Bacchus has broken free of his paddock in order to check out the noise coming from the house. Once spotted, he nonchalantly dips his head and begins nibbling from the vegie patch as if to reassure us he is not sticky-beaking.

Bacchus loves a game. He loves to butt and to test his strength. Doug happily engages in his games, enjoying testing his strength too. Boys will be boys, I guess. It is obvious that Bacchus respects Doug's alpha male status – Doug can now yell out to him from the back veranda if he has broken into a paddock where he doesn't belong and he will hurriedly return home.

His games quickly became too boisterous for me and I had to put a stop to them. Bacchus would always wait for me at the gate in the afternoon to accompany me up to the feed shed. He didn't like it at all if I acknowledged the sheep, butting me or placing himself across my path if I tried to head in their direction.

He also loves nothing better than to push his head into the generous proportions of my bottom. That would be fine, except for his magnificent horns, which sometimes find their way to places that cause considerable discomfort.

These days he seems content if I throw my arms around him for a hug whilst rubbing his chest. I think we both enjoy the experience.

I did earn an unexpected butt recently, though. With the lush summer pastures to feed from, I was reminded by an old farmer to keep an eye on the goat and sheep for scours, an unpleasant *tummy upset. That afternoon, after a hug, I decided to check for the yogurty discharge from Bacchus' back passage. I lifted his tail and bent down to look. I was rewarded with a quick, sharp bunt and a look that clearly said, "How Dare You!"*

I love Bacchus's bleat which can be quite loud when he is on supervisory duties. However, there is nothing sadder than his pathetic, "Mah! Mah!" when he is in trouble, such as being immobilised by his whiskers entwined in the barbed wire fence or too many raindrops messing up his usually dry, comfortable pen.

We love to see Bacchus enjoying his retirement. Whether playing with Doug or inspecting our activities, he makes us laugh.

What a gift he has been.

These words seem to encapsulate my goats' attitude to food and people, as corroborated by Trish and Helen.

> *"I don't often stop to smell the flowers, but when I do, there's none left for you."*
>
> Source unknown

Pamela's first sheep – a freshly shorn Agnes with Madelaine and Bunter

Bunter the ram in a less 'bunterish' moment

Pamela's later sheep – Medea and Jason and their son Festes, after they were relocated to Eewah Vale

The three sheep and Bacchus the bossy goat, refusing to be left out, at Eewah Vale

"This is the life." – The sheep at Eehwah Vale

Ariadne the goat, who was devoted to Dionysus

Bacchus the goat – "The bougainvillea leaf is just out of reach, how annoying!"

Bacchus, an Eastern type of goat common in Syria, Lebanon and Cyprus. Where is everyone Surely it's teatime

Pamela with Ariadne and Bacchus

Bacchus, Mr Bossy Boots, at Eewah Vale

Bacchus showing his goats' eyes with the rectangular iris – "If you don't hurry with my tea, I'll do a 'Bunter' on you!"

Chapter 6
Brief Encounters

"When I look into the eyes of an animal, I don't see an animal, I see a living being. I see a friend. I feel a 'soul'."
Antony Douglas Williams

Cockroaches and Ants

I must admit there are two creatures which do not evoke the above sentiments in me. So let us dispose of them first. They are cockroaches, especially those large flying ones with the white circle on their heads, and black biting ants.

From a small child, I have been frightened, indeed terrified by cockroaches. It dates from an experience when I was about two years old. I slept on a bed on the veranda and in the days before fly screens, I had a mosquito net. A large flying cockroach penetrated the net. I remember crying out for Mum, but I was going through a phase of not wanting to go to sleep.

Mum thought that was part of my strategy and would not come. By the time she realised there was a real problem, my fear of cockroaches had become a lifetime obsession.

For years, I could not go to our outside toilet unless Dad inspected it carefully for signs of waving antennae, and he sprayed them with Radox if necessary. During the war, even this solution was not possible. These days, I can get close enough to spray them but now I feel rather sorry for them, as they lie on their backs waving their legs feebly. Poor things – *they* are suffering.

Black ants are a different matter. I am not afraid of them, but of what damage they do to my power points. They have shorted out my TV and a number of other points. It is a mystery, what is so attractive about *my* power points. What is more, they leave a painful bite. I spray them without compunction.

Chickens, Geese and a Duck

> *"Regard it as just as desirable to build a chicken house as to build a cathedral."*
> Frank Lloyd Wright

I cannot really argue that my relationship with hens was a brief encounter because I had poultry for many years. However, my encounters with individual hens were brief. Breeders, eyeing their own profits, developed a breed which by fiddling with their genes, laid large eggs. Unfortunately, after a brief laying life, the hens succumbed to egg peritonitis. This was very painful. The only solution was to euthanise. I gradually replaced these early red hens with heritage types. I kept a rooster for many years until neighbours complained, and my hens and roosters produced occasional clutches of chickens.

My first 'chooks' were given to me by my students. One Easter, they presented me with a large Easter egg and three-day old chickens. Chickens are very difficult to sex, so as they grew, it was obvious that two were roosters.

I named them Nero and Tiberius after two of the more unpopular Roman emperors. Because Nero was white with some reddy-brown splashes on his wings and his name-sake was purported to be red-headed, it seemed suitable. Tiberius was white.

Nero was very affectionate and knew his name. When I called, he came running up followed by the several wives I had acquired for him. Tiberius was very jealous. On one occasion I was nursing Nero, and Tiberius jumped up to peck Nero, but inflicted a painful wound on the back of my hand instead. The next morning my hand was badly swollen so I went to the doctor near school. When asked how I acquired the wound, I explained the incident. The doctor gave me a strange look.

I was able to find a home for Tiberius on a friend's farm, as two competing roosters was not a good situation.

When driving one day I saw a little hen fall from a transporter bound for the abattoirs. I picked her up and found she had hardly any feathers and a very pale comb. With good food and healthy outdoor living, she became one of my best layers and lived very much longer than my red hens.

There is no sound more calming than that of contented hens clucking gently in the sun as they peck the ground for food.

I used to feed a friend's animals when she was away. They included poultry and geese, which were quite friendly. I could not understand why Mum, when she came to help me, would not come in to close the gate to shut the geese up. The only creatures I ever saw Mum fear were geese. She explained that when working for her father she used to take the mail to the Moorooka Post Office. Invariably she was attacked by a flock of geese. They are very effective 'watchdogs' but should have been restrained, and not allowed on the public footpath.

Geese, sacred to the goddess Juno, were credited with saving Rome from the Gauls in 390BC. The soldiers guarding the Capitoline Hill, Rome's fortress, slept through the invaders' approach, and so did the dogs. The geese attached to the temple of Juno set up such a commotion, that the invaders were intercepted and Rome was saved. Once a year, a goose draped in a purple robe, was carried through the streets of Rome in triumph, while a dog was hanged.

While I was feeding Denise's animals, I found one of the roosters drowned in the horse's trough. Not very optimistically, I held him upside down to get rid of some of the water, and then applied mouth to beak resuscitation. Miraculously he recovered, and I asked Denise if I could have him. He was a handsome fellow and I had him for many years. I also applied the same treatment to a number of birds hit by cars and my attempts were often successful.

A former student of mine once gave me a duck which she had rescued from the university pond. The helpless drake was badly crippled and it was hard for him to get food. I installed a paddle pool for him and made sure he was properly protected when he was eating. He was an 'ugly duckling' amongst the hens and he lived happily for some years.

> *"The only thing that ever sat its way to success was the hen."*
>
> Sarah Brown

A Possum

Unfortunately, no one seems to have a suitable quote about possums, so I shall contribute one.

> *'A possum on the roof at night is an annoyance, but a possum as a very independent pet is a joy.'*

When entering the feed house one morning, I glanced up to see a ring-tail possum resting on a beam in a space under the roof. He was there for the next few days, so I decided to make his resting place more luxurious.

I asked my neighbour to provide two boxes – one with a shade-cloth for the summer, and one without for the cold weather. Between the two boxes was a board with a container for water and one for food.

I started to feed him each morning with slices of carrot, apple, sweet potato, pawpaw and banana.

Each morning he was there, holding out his paws for the food. This continued for over a year, but one day he was not there and I never saw him again. He was probably killed by a car or a dog.

I was so sad – I felt we had become friends and he trusted me.

Lucy the Wallaby

*"Though the way of the swagman is mostly up-hill,
There are joys to be found on the wallaby still."*
From On the Wallaby by Henry Lawson

A wallaby's life seems to be a life of leisure. My next-door neighbour but one, the same neighbour whose horse played with my dog Sheba, had a wallaby called Lucy. Lucy used to come over and swing on the clothes hanging on the Hills Hoist washing line. She would hop around and lift her back feet up, using the momentum to have a lovely swing, as if on a merry-go-round. She spent a lot of time bouncing along at my property. Early one Sunday morning while I was still in bed, she came into the bedroom, bounced on the bed and settled down for a sleep. She had absolutely no fear of humans.

She did not return home one day, and Liz, the owner, went searching in the bush and found she had been shot. It upsets me when I think of it and Liz was heartbroken.

Snakes and Lizards

"A snake attacks only in self-defence. Don't get too close. Use your common sense."
Australian folklore

Because I live on acreage, I often see snakes, mostly pythons, but occasionally little tree or grass snakes, and once a very venomous red-bellied black. I do not fear snakes but use my 'common sense'.

One night I heard a banging on the screen door from the laundry which faced the garden. I looked through the glass in the back door for the source. I was concerned for a possible human intruder.

Later, I took the dog out for his final 'wee' and came face to face with a very large python. He was shedding his skin by rubbing it on the trellis I had over the two doors. I bobbed down to pass beneath him. The dog did not notice. The next morning his discarded skin was on the trellis and the snake was resting from his labours there too. He was in a position where I could touch him, so I did so. He was warm and smooth; not at all slippery.

Snakes' movements are so sinuous and graceful. I do not see many such beautiful creatures these days. My neighbours seem to think the only good snake is a dead snake.

Only once did I get a wildlife officer to remove a snake, and that was when he was sharing the feed house with the possum. The python might have wanted to have a tasty treat of possum.

My mother, having been a country girl in Kin Kin, had no fear of snakes. I came home one day to find my cousin, Winifred, standing on a chair, quaking with fear. Mum was standing between the veranda door and the rest of the house, clapping her hands at a red-bellied black snake.

"Don't let it get into the house Pamela. We will never get it out." It was within about two feet of Mum.

The snake slithered off under the house. I was relieved until I remembered Mum's cats liked to sleep there. Down I went to check on their safety. The snake had disappeared so the cats were safe. Winifred never visited Mum nor me again at home; we had to go to her.

On this occasion, I did not follow my own advice; that to snakes, we humans are large predators, from which they wish to escape. They are more frightened of us, than we are of them.

As well as snakes, I have many lizards, large and small, on the property.

There are blue-tongue lizards which move so sinuously, skinks and frill-necked lizards, which doze in the sun on my gate post. They all bring pleasure, though my neighbour who is a recent immigrant is terrified of all wildlife larger than an ant. I am of the opinion that he should be living on the fifth floor of a high-rise building.

All lizards bring me pleasure.

Pamela Davenport

Rabbits and Guinea Pigs

"Rabbits are like people; they have a way of finding people who need them and filling an emptiness we did not know we had."

Anonymous

The keeping of rabbits is illegal in Queensland and there is even a rabbit-proof fence to exclude wild rabbits. Unfortunately, domestic rabbits are included in this ban.

A friend who had fallen in love with a white rabbit when visiting Sydney, phoned me in a panic. She had brought that rabbit home without realising the consequences of a substantial fine. Would I take him?

Since I lived in an isolated position without neighbours, I agreed. I had him castrated and named him Peter and he lived his illegal life for many years.

After Peter had died, my vet called about a client, who had phoned him to say that he had seen a white rabbit loose in the yard of a house which was up for sale. The client asked whether the vet could come to collect it. He did so, and he asked me to give it a home. I agreed, being rather anxious, since I was no longer rather isolated. Sadly, she was heavily pregnant and later gave birth to many kittens, all of which died. She also died, so she probably had some underlying disease. I was glad I had tried to give her a happy home.

My experience of guinea pigs started in my childhood, when I was seven years old and attending Yeronga State School. I was told by my schoolmate David Cilento of the renowned Cilento family in Brisbane, that he had pet guinea pigs. I had longed for guinea pigs, so in great excitement, I walked with David to see them. This expedition took me further away from home so I was very late walking the mile home. Mum was frantic. My parents decided to allow me to have guinea pigs of my own.

They were called Snowball, who was all white, and Elsie, who was brown, black and white. Dad made a luxurious home for them with chicken wire in front, a door to allow for cleaning the cage, a miniature house with a veranda for their sleeping quarters, and some straw for the bottom of the cage. They were very happy in their lovely cage. We researched their diets carefully. Cabbage was a no-no and too much lettuce is not good for guinea pigs' digestion. Carrots were good and not very green lucerne.

Unfortunately, there was one disaster we had not foreseen; when Dad was cleaning out the cage, he placed the girls under a sieve on the grass. The sun was strong and both died of exposure. I was very upset.

The next guinea pig, which I acquired years later, was a companion for my rabbit. Dante the dog loved them both and the guinea pig lived for several years before dying of old age. I had learned a valuable lesson with the loss of Snowball and Elsie.

Little Critters

"All creatures great and small, the Lord God made them all..."
English Hymn

In my childhood, keeping silkworms was very popular, and with Dad's encouragement and the willingness of neighbours to supply me with mulberry leaves, I had silkworms every year, which I kept in a shoebox. Dad, who had silkworms as a child, taught me how to spin their silk. When the worms reached the chrysalis stage, we spun the silk, twisting it into small skeins which I still have as bookmarks. After five years of keeping silkworms each year, I came home one day and discovered to my great sorrow that ants had attacked my silkworms and all my little friends were dead.

I never kept silkworms again, but when I was in Paphos, Cyprus, I went to the Folk Museum and there were hundreds of small paper bags attached to the wall, one silkworm in each, and the sound of their munching was almost deafening. Perhaps if mine had been managed in this way, they would have escaped the ants. I am not, however, sure of Mum's reaction to that solution. Dad had reared his silkworms in paper bags on the wall as a child, but his mother was not as houseproud as Mum.

I have never been frightened of spiders. Indeed, when I was shut by accident in the wood box beside the woodstove in Kin Kin, I was frightened by the possibility of there being cockroaches but not the certainty of there being Huntsmen or Tarantulas. These large spiders amongst the wood were a curiosity for me as a six-year-old.

I have many spiders that build their webs from tree to tree. I try to avoid walking into their webs both for my sake and for the spiders'. They do so much good in keeping flies and other unwanted insects at bay. Sometimes a large spider will find its way into the house. Spiders inside the house do not seem to live very long, with few other insects able to penetrate the flyscreens. I would never kill a spider. There is a simple, safe way to remove it, and carry it outside.

In Cyprus one day, I was in the studio of Sarah, the archaeologist's wife. She had an aversion to all spiders. She was terrified of a very large spider, probably a Huntsman. I removed it by simply placing a glass container over it and sliding a sheet of paper under the glass. I then turned the glass over and put my hand over it and carried it outside to release the spider.

Spiders are so good for the environment. They are worth saving.

I cannot argue that I have a relationship with termites, but on one occasion I thought I was doing them a favour.

On the farm in Kin Kin, in one of the paddocks there were several termite mounds. I used to enjoy watching them busily hurrying about their business. I thought it must have been difficult for them to penetrate their mounds through small openings, so decided to dig deep passageways to help their comings and goings. The next morning, they had filled the passages in. I tried once more, but when the passages were filled in, I realised Nature knew best!

Bush Sounds

"Carols of bush birds rising and falling..."
From 'Carol of the Birds' by John Wheeler Melody by William James

Because I live in such an isolated place, I am constantly surrounded by the sounds of the bush. It gives me great pleasure to hear the cicadas in the heat of the day and myriad of bird sounds from early in the morning till late in the afternoon. These include galas, rosellas, the occasional white cockatoo, butcher birds with their beautiful song, magpies and peewees. The willy-wagtails seem to have been displaced by native noisy miners due to landscape clearing, as well as by Indian mynas which have become very common. There are also kookaburras and though rare, the occasional whip-bird, whose cry is like the crack of a whip.

Once I found an Indian myna drowned in the horse trough. I was very distressed because my attempt to resuscitate by mouth to beak did not work. My friend Anne, who was staying with me, said that they were a pest, and I should not be sorry. I, however, felt the poor thing had suffered, whether it was a pest or not.

A positive outcome of this method occurred on the way to church one day, when I saw some crested pigeons beside the road that had flown across in front of a car. I massaged their little chests and tried mouth to beak to get them to breathe again. I had a box in the car and I put two or three of them in the box where it was dark and quiet, and when I arrived home, opened the box and they flew away.

"No matter how few possessions you have, loving wildlife and nature will make you rich beyond measure."
Paul Oxton

Postscript

"We call them dumb animals and so they are, for they cannot tell us how they feel, but they do not suffer less because they have no words."
Anna Sewell

While writing this book, I have been able to remember the stories of my experiences with animals, most happy but invariably, some sad. Writing has also focused my mind on my philosophy towards animals.

The Bible states two very different views of Man's relationship with animals.

In the Old Testament, Genesis I:28, God is recorded as saying that after the creation of Adam and Eve, God blessed them and said to them, 'Be fruitful and fill the earth and subdue it and have dominion over it, over the fish of the sea, birds of the air and every living thing; every creature that crawls upon the earth.'

In the New Testament, Matthew 10:29, Jesus says, 'Are not two sparrows sold for a penny? Yet not one of them will fall to the ground outside your Father's care.'

There seems to be a dichotomy here, or at least I believe Genesis may have been misunderstood. 'Have dominion' does not mean in my view, exploitation. In countries which do not exploit their subjects but hopefully make benign decisions for their wellbeing, there is no exploitation.

This 'should' be the case regarding Man's relationship with animals too. One situation which pains me is people's view of feral animals. They are spoken of with such scorn, and treated with such hatred, and there is complete denial of their suffering when slaughtered. Who brought them here? Our forebears, both distant and more recent, brought them to Australia for their own advantage, only sadly to become an environmental disaster. These include rabbits, cane toads, foxes, camels, and even donkeys are amongst these animals that are classed as feral.

It is worth contemplating that loneliness in people, caused by lockdowns of the population, is causing people to turn to the companionship of animals. Animal shelters have been emptied. I fear that when life returns to normal, some of those same animals will find themselves back in animal shelters because their short-term owners no longer want or need them. Some will be discarded like old pairs of shoes or worn-out toasters.

I end these reflections with the words of Mahatma Gandhi.

> *"The greatness of a nation and its moral progress can be judged by the way its animals are treated."*
> Mahatma Gandhi

Nero and two of his wives – "I'm lord of all I survey."

The red hen family – "This breed I would avoid at all costs because they are condemned to a painful death."

One of the many native creatures on Pamela's property at Kuraby. This frill-necked lizard used to doze on the gate post in the sun.

About the Author

Pamela Davenport is a former teacher of History at Somerville House, a Brisbane Independent Girls' School, who attended the school in the 1950s and taught there for 45 years. She has a passion for History, both Modern, which she taught for several years, and Ancient History, in which she has several post-graduate degrees. She has worked as a volunteer archaeologist in Paphos Cyprus for 25 years. Now retired, she maintained her love of History for many more years teaching at U3A. Throughout her life, she has maintained a great love for animals, and has raised dogs, cats, donkeys, goats, ponies, sheep, chickens, and more besides, entertaining her generations of students and friends with their anecdotes.

www.ingramcontent.com/pod-product-compliance
Lightning Source LLC
Chambersburg PA
CBHW062102290426
44110CB00022B/2686